Elizabeth has given us both a commentary and a devotional on Genesis 1–3. Though this may be familiar territory for some, readers will be truly inspired as she takes us deeper into these chapters than most of us have gone before. I hope many groups will study this together and be inspired in community to live out their gifts in the image of God.

—**Wendy Alsup**, Author, *Companions in Suffering: Comfort for Times of Loss and Loneliness*

Sometimes, you really do need to back up and start at the very beginning. Sometimes, knowing who you are begins with remembering *whose* you are. In *Freedom to Flourish*, Garn calls us to remember that the joy and fulfillment we seek cannot be uncoupled from our calling as God's image bearers. Offering readers a better story than traditionalist gender tropes or the try-harder-do-better mantras of secularism, she invites us into true freedom—the freedom of becoming our truest selves through Christ.

—**Hannah Anderson**, Author, *Made for More: An Invitation to Live in God's Image*

It's not every day that you read a book and sense God causing your heart to feel simultaneously rested *and* stirred toward loving action. This is the twofold impact of *Freedom to Flourish*: Elizabeth Garn has taken a careful look at Genesis 1–3 and in these pages shares the fruit of long hours spent gazing at Christ and what it means for us to be image bearers of God through him. If you're tired, bent down under shame, or just plain confused about what it means to be a faithful Christian woman, read this book and allow God to draw you closer to himself, then compel you outward . . . to flourish and rest through life as a loved image bearer.

—**Ellen Mary Dykas**, Women's Ministry Director, Harvest USA

Who am I? This is one of life's most important questions. For many women, including myself, the answers we've heard have only left us confused, unanchored, and empty. In *Freedom to Flourish*, Elizabeth Garn takes us through Genesis 1–3 and shows us the glorious purpose for which we were created. Sisters, read this book with joy as you receive the gift of purpose, crafted for you by the Maker himself.

—**Christina Fox**, Counselor; Writer; Retreat Speaker; Author, *A Holy Fear: Trading Lesser Fears for the Fear of the Lord*

Elizabeth Garn's wise, careful exposition of Genesis 1–3 leads us to see the story of creation with new eyes. Her lively, well-organized prose provides fresh insights about what it means to be an image bearer; how sin destroys but God binds up and restores; and how God calls us to join him in his work of redemption and community. *Freedom to Flourish* is infused with grace and the soul-rest that our creative, redeeming, restoring God provides.

—**Maria Garriott**, Author, *A Thousand Resurrections: An Urban Spiritual Journey*

In a world where self-determination and independence are the air we breathe, *Freedom to Flourish* is a life-giving invitation to be rather than do. Its pages bring a fresh perspective of what it looks like for women to thrive in their creation design.

—**Karen Hodge**, Coordinator of Women's Ministries, Presbyterian Church in America (PCA); Author, *Transformed: Life-Taker to Life-Giver* and *Life-Giving Leadership*

Like an excellent optician, Elizabeth Garn accurately calibrates our vision so that we can more clearly see what it means for Christian women to be image bearers of God, who is our Creator and Redeemer. Centering both our identity and our purpose in this clarified reality, Garn enthusiastically calls Christian women to renewed engagement in a life that wholeheartedly promotes flourishing in the world around us.

—**Stephanie O. Hubach**, Research Fellow in Disability Ministries, Covenant Theological Seminary

So many books for Christian women focus on the roles we inhabit. While that can be helpful for navigating the complexities of life, what happens when we no longer inhabit that role? What does the Bible say to me if I'm single or no longer married? Who am I if I am not a mother or I find myself an empty nester? Though roles shift and change over time, our identity is secure. Are we preparing women to think outside these roles and embrace a calling that moves beyond what fills our day-to-day life? Elizabeth Garn does an excellent job of reminding us of what we were created for. She encourages our hearts with the truth that God has called us to be his image bearers, to fill the earth with his glory as imitators of our great God. We were made to create, restore, and rescue. What a high calling! I truly appreciate Elizabeth's care for all women in every age and stage of life. She speaks with compassion and teaches our hearts to embrace the One who created us in his image and likeness for his great purposes.

—**Abby Ross Hutto**, Director of Spiritual Formation, Story Presbyterian Church, Westerville, Ohio; Author, *God For Us: Discovering the Heart of the Father through the Life of the Son*

Freedom to Flourish is a breath of fresh air for any woman who feels exhausted from the try-harder-do-more pressures of life. Elizabeth Garn carefully explores the first three chapters of Genesis and unpacks the good news of what they reveal about our identity and purpose. Writing with biblical wisdom and insight, Garn warmly invites women to rest in God as they faithfully fulfill their calling.

—**Melissa Kruger**, Author; Director of Women's Initiatives, The Gospel Coalition

Genesis 1–2 is often described like a symphony, and reading this book is like sitting next to a friend who understands the piece and points out how each note sings of God's grace and love, personally inviting you to enter the music at a life-changing level! In these pages, Elizabeth honestly shares from her own struggles and invites us to reconsider our calling as image bearers, lovingly exposing misconceptions and constraints so that we are freed to glory in who the Lord is and to embrace our purpose to reflect him in the world.

—**Meaghan May**, Women's Ministry Regional Advisor for the Northeast, PCA Discipleship Ministries; Trainer and Local Network Leader, Parakaleo

Freedom to Flourish is a must-read for men who love Jesus, the Bible, and the church. Elizabeth Garn makes a compelling, fair, in-depth biblical case for what it means to bear God's image and the implications and emancipations that image bearing ought to bring to our daily lives. This book gives men an opportunity to listen in, respectfully, and to learn and to grow in empathy for many seldom-discussed struggles commonly experienced by half of the body of Christ. These pages contain insight and biblical exposition that men as well as women in the church would do well to study, discuss, and absorb.

—**Paul May**, Church Planter and Senior Pastor, King's Cross Church, Ashburn, Virginia

Through a faithful and challenging interpretation of Genesis 1–3, Elizabeth Garn offers an insightful and hope-giving understanding of God's design for human flourishing, the effects of sin, and the restoration offered in the gospel. Both men and women will be instructed and edified by *Freedom to Flourish*.

—**Eric Schumacher**, Coauthor, *Worthy: Celebrating the Value of Women*; Cohost, *Worthy* podcast with Elyse Fitzpatrick

Have you ever felt worn out or confused about what it looks like to be a "woman of God"? If so, you will welcome the gospel-rich refreshment and sound theology of Elizabeth Garn's *Freedom to Flourish*. Join Elizabeth in discovering God's delight in you as his beloved creation. Rest in the sure hope she shares: even though you may still struggle with sin, you have been restored in Christ, and he is making you more loving and more lovely every day. Pick up this book, and discover your freedom to flourish in God's design.

—**Elizabeth Reynolds Turnage**, Bible Teacher; Gospel Coach; Author, *From Recovery to Restoration: 60 Meditations for Finding Peace and Hope in Crisis*

Elizabeth Garn provides a compassionate and winsome voice for those struggling with their calling as Christian women. Her focus on the image of God as a truly holistic call is a welcome antidote to voices and assumptions that seek to shrink its scope. She rightfully insists that women as well as men are made in God's likeness to serve him and their neighbors in all sorts of ways. And best of all, she reminds readers repeatedly that their worth in God's sight does not come from their own efforts but as a gift from him, who bestows on us all the privilege of imaging our Creator.

—**David VanDrunen**, Robert B. Strimple Professor of Systematic Theology and Christian Ethics, Westminster Seminary California

FREEDOM *to* FLOURISH

FREEDOM
to
FLOURISH

The Rest God Offers
in the Purpose He Gives You

ELIZABETH GARN

PUBLISHING
P.O. BOX 817 • PHILLIPSBURG • NEW JERSEY 08865-0817

Printed in the United States of America

Library of Congress Cataloging-in-Publication Data

Names: Garn, Elizabeth, author.
Title: Freedom to flourish : the rest God offers in the purpose he gives you / Elizabeth Garn.
Description: Phillipsburg, New Jersey : P&R Publishing, [2021] | Summary: "So many women are exhausted because they think their purpose is rooted in what they do. Instead, it's rooted in who God is. Learn how we flourish as his image-bearers"-- Provided by publisher.
Identifiers: LCCN 2020045439 | ISBN 9781629956084 (paperback) | ISBN 9781629956091 (epub) | ISBN 9781629956107 (mobi)
Subjects: LCSH: Women--Religious aspects--Christianity. | Women in Christianity.
Classification: LCC BT704 .G37 2021 | DDC 248.8/43--dc23
LC record available at https://lccn.loc.gov/2020045439

To my husband, Steve.
There is no one else I would rather walk through this life with.
Thank you for loving me well and living the
image of God in my life.

And to my children.
You are a constant source of encouragement and enthusiasm,
and I thank God every day that he let me be your mom!

CONTENTS

INTRODUCTION

A woman of God is . . .

> . . . *calm and quiet. She speaks with wisdom and faithfulness. She is gentle. Kind. Meek. She doesn't gossip, doesn't quarrel. . . . She pretty much doesn't speak at all . . .*

The words came, unbidden, forming a list that echoed through my mind.

> . . . *she is pure and chaste. She is never tempted. She doesn't sin. She doesn't think about sex. Doesn't want it. Would never have it. Until she's married. Then . . . she keeps her husband satisfied, loves sex, and pretty much wants it all the time.*

> *She is married. She cares for her husband. She cares for the house. She does the laundry, the dishes; she cooks, she cleans, she has a career, and she stays home. She studies her Bible every day . . . every morning . . . every night. She sort-of never even goes to bed.*

Each word, each contradiction, brought fresh condemnation to my heart, but try as I might, I couldn't make them stop.

> *She is a mother. She loves her children, is never annoyed by them, never wants time away from them, and gives thanks every time she hears, "Mommy . . . Mommy . . . Mommy . . . Mommy . . ." She home-schools. She private schools. She public schools. She formula feeds. She*

breastfeeds. She cooks organic. She grows organic. She wears organic. . . . Is that even a thing?

She does it all. She is practically perfect in every way, and she's probably writing a blog about it too . . .

And that's when I started crying in earnest.

I sat on my bed, crumpled over, a mess of tears and mascara. All the things I was supposed to do to be a godly woman ran through my head with the thundering, repetitive crash of a sledgehammer on drywall. The force of the words ripped at my heart and tore away my hopes of ever being a "real" woman of God. They left me a shell of crumbling two-by-fours and destroyed plaster cleverly disguised as a young woman, a new wife.

I was in college when I got married. We had the overwhelming support of our parents and pastors, but our friends were shocked. I was still a student; why would I want to add "wife" to the mix? Why would I even want to try? But Steve and I were best friends and madly in love and couldn't think of any good reasons to wait any longer to start our lives together. I had all these picture-perfect ideas about the kind of marriage we would have and the type of wife I was going to be: the kind of wife good Christian women were *supposed* to be. I was going to do everything good Christian women did and would prove that I could handle this! Because I could. I knew that if I worked hard enough, I could do it.

As soon as I said, "I do," I started *doing* everything I thought I should do to be a good Christian woman. I got up early and went to bed late. I cooked three meals a day. I read my Bible. I cleaned. I did the laundry. I finished my degree, spent time with my new husband, led Bible studies, volunteered at church . . . and then I cried. Which is saying a lot for me. In all the years Steve and I dated, he had seen me cry only one other time. I'm not a crier. I'm a doer. After all, there's no time for emotions when your goal is to be a Proverbs 31 woman! At least, that's what I thought.

It took one year. One year into our marriage and I was ready to give up, throw in the towel, and go to bed. Oh no, I wasn't giving up on our relationship. I didn't want out, I wanted a break . . . and possibly a good night's sleep and some chocolate cake thrown in for good measure. What was wrong? I was not the perfect wife. No, it was deeper than that: I was a lousy Christian woman. I was sure of it. If it were just about being a wife, I might have been able to cope a little bit longer. But this was more than that. All those things I was supposed to do, all those expectations, had become intertwined in my mind with who I was as a Christian and as a woman. Failing to do all the right things was equal to failing as a person. It wasn't just about my role anymore; it was about my identity.

I grew up in the church; I'd heard all about biblical femininity or womanhood or whatever you want to call it. I'd been to the retreats, Bible studies, conferences, and Sunday school classes. I studied Ruth and Hannah and Mary and, of course, that infamous woman at the end of Proverbs. I thought I knew what it meant to be a woman of God, but the truth was, so much of what I had internalized for all those years was confusing and conflicting. I had come to believe that the Christian life was about what I *did*. Holiness amounted to doing more and trying harder and running myself ragged in between.

As a young woman, I didn't want to think about all the ways I was falling short, but I also didn't know how to stop that list from repeating in my head over and over and over again. It was all I knew about the Christian life, about God's plan for me. So I clung to it, hoping that I had done enough. Hoping I was enough. Oh sure, I knew God loved me. I knew Jesus had died for me and saved me. I knew I was God's child. But sitting there I felt lost, alone, and completely unsure.

Have you ever felt like that?

Many Christian women have heard messages about our worth, our value . . . our purpose. Maybe not as overtly as I had, or maybe even more so. And as a result, many women in the church today are under the impression that the heart of God's plan for us is lists and doing. We have been told or have come to believe that if we try hard enough, we can measure up; that if we have enough children, we have arrived; that if we do the right studies and read the right books and volunteer more, we will have done enough. It's a belief that lies deeply ingrained in us, sometimes without our even knowing it's there, and it's a belief that is wounding the hearts of women in the church. When we don't have a solid understanding of who God created us to be and how he planned for us to live out our purpose together, we will flounder and create plans for ourselves instead.

We long for lives of meaning but are inundated by failures instead. Our hearts cry out for more, so we scrounge through the Bible and search for any indication that we have a higher purpose than simply doing. We cling to other accounts in the Bible of women of worth, and we study their lives hoping for a clue to our own value. It becomes easy, then, to read about the woman in Proverbs 31 and see only a list of things godly women ought to do. We read about Ruth and cling to the idea that if we just stay faithful, we'll have done enough. But just in case, let's do more. Without even realizing it, we've created a works-based pseudo-salvation that's leaving us hurting, discouraged, and exhausted. Not that our work will save us—we know or have heard that our salvation is through faith alone in Christ alone and by grace alone. But we think our role is rooted in our work. Or even worse, our value is based there. We've misunderstood the truth of God's plan for us, and it's left us exhausted, isolated, and drowning in shame.

It was that deep-rooted but unrealized belief that my purpose was rooted in what I did that led me to that moment all those years ago when I sat on my bed and wept. I thought God's plan for me was all about me and what I was doing, and that misunderstanding was crushing me. I had no idea that his plan didn't start and end with *me* but was all about *him*. I didn't realize that it wasn't about doing more to somehow qualify as a woman of God; it was about living out his image on the earth. It was about bringing flourishing to the world around me.

I don't know if you can relate to any of that. But if you can—if you've ever felt the pull between being the woman you are and being the woman you think you're supposed to be, if you've ever believed that the heart of God's plan for us was doing more and trying harder—then this book is for you. I spent years and years tangled in the idea that I needed to measure up to the women around me, that I needed to fit in and look the part and check the boxes all to somehow prove that I loved God enough, that I was godly enough. I didn't understand who I was created to be or how I was to live that out, and, as a result, I was left sinking in shame instead. But that is not God's plan for us. His plan is not for shame but for freedom, not for comparison but for flourishing; his plan is that we be his image.

And that's what this book is all about: image bearing. Not the image of the women around us, though, or the lists we've created in our heads. No, this is a book about what it really, truly means to be an image bearer of God and the amazing, life-changing, heart-healing freedom that we've been given to live out our purpose today. It's a book about being freed from our misunderstandings, from the shame and comparison that bind us so tightly. Because we weren't created to be just "good Christian women"—we were created to be image bearers of God. My prayer is that the pages of this book will bring you hope in your own life as you come to see, maybe even for the first time, who it is God created you to be, the amazing purpose he created you with, and the immense freedom that comes from living it out.

If you're a notetaker or outline sort of person (I am, so I'm right there with you), you'll see from the table of contents that the book is divided into two parts: Created and Restored. In the first part, we'll look at God's purpose for creating us and his plan for us to live as his image bearers on the earth. In the second, we'll look at what went wrong in the garden and how God is restoring all things to himself, even his very image in us.

To do that, we're going to go back to the very beginning and dig deep into the creation account. We're going to sit in Genesis 1–3 and soak in the promises that were spoken in those first moments of creation. We're going to rest in the hope of who God is and his amazing plan for us. And then we're going to look at what all of that means for us now. Because God's purpose for us really is bigger than fake smiles and to-do lists, and his call to us is more freeing and more amazing than many of us have ever realized.

We don't have to live tangled up in confusion and misunderstandings anymore—we have been freed to live as the image of God!

PART 1

CREATED

1

THE LOVE OF GOD

The earth was without form and void, and darkness
was over the face of the deep. And the Spirit of God was
hovering over the face of the waters. (Gen. 1:2)

Then God said, "Let us make man." (Gen. 1:26)

"Do you know what?" I looked down at the tiny button nose and the impish grin on my daughter's sleepy face and smiled.

"What?"

"I love you!"

She sighed and flopped her arms on the fluffy comforter that was tucked up around her. "Mommy! I know that! You tell me every day!"

She was right. This was a common conversation in our house—one that was repeated over and over again in different ways and at different times but always with the same message: you are unconditionally loved. Her eyes met mine as she waited for what always came next.

"And is there anything you could ever do to make me love you any less? To lose even a single drop of my love?"

"Nope!"

"What if you said not-nice things? Or were really mean to your brother and sister? What if you smashed all my stuff and told lots of lies?"

She looked suitably horrified—these were pretty big infractions—but she laughed along with me and shook her head.

"And is there anything you could ever do to make me love you *more*?"

This one stumped her. It was a new addition to our script, an addition that I realized in that moment was just as important as everything that we had said thus far.

Her eyebrows pulled together, and she tilted her head to the side. "No . . . ?"

"What if you made your bed every day and cleaned up your room perfectly? What if you helped to set the table and colored me a picture every day? Would that make me love you more?"

"No," she said, a bit more confidently this time.

"What if you were the nicest girl in the world and always obeyed the first time, every time, and with a happy heart? Would I love you more?"

"Nope!"

"You're right. Why do you think that is?"

She shrugged.

"Because you have all my love right now! All of it! You can't ever lose it, and you can't earn any more because you already have every last bit of it!"

There were tickles and giggles and hugs at that point, and the conversation moved on. Eventually, after goodnight kisses and bedtime prayers, I slipped out of her room and closed the door softly behind me. Standing in the hall, I let the import of those words sink into my heart as well.

I've always known about unconditional love, especially the unconditional love of God. After all, "Jesus Loves Me" is practically required learning for kids who grow up in the church. But while I had known that God loved me and that I couldn't lose any of that love, I had never thought about how I couldn't earn *more* of it either. And while I would love to say that fact was obvious (salvation is a free gift, after all), the truth is, I was living like it wasn't and like I could.

This idea of earning God's love goes way back for me. I was a churchgoing girl from the beginning, and I took wearing my Sunday best, putting my quarter in the offering jar, and reading my Bible a little bit every day very seriously. As a teen my attempts to earn God's love morphed into having official "quiet times," attending youth group regularly, and listening to only "Christian" music. As an adult, I tried to make myself look as godly as the women around me—leading ministries, attending conferences, posting verses on my Facebook wall. All of those are fine things—good, even—but when you do them because you're hoping to earn favor with God, they become less acts of worship and more like bargaining chips. I wasn't worried that God was going to turn his back on me, but I was worried that if I didn't do enough, I would be missing out. Missing his blessings. Missing his presence. Missing his love.

For much of my life, I have operated, sometimes without even realizing it, as if I could earn more of God's love. As if the love he loved me with at the cross was just a baseline amount and more love was available for those who worked hard enough. That if I was good enough, life would be better, or if I tried hard enough or prayed hard enough, things would go well and he would be happy with me. But the truth is, children of God can't earn more of his love any more than we can lose it, which is to say, not at all.

When we don't understand the depth of God's love for us, when we think or feel like we need to do certain things to earn more of his love or live in fear that we might lose some, we've missed the heart of both who he created us to be and how he planned for us to live that out. It's a confusing, exhausting, depressing way to live. This misunderstanding pushes us into shame and prevents us from living in the type of community we so desperately need.

But God does not operate that way, and this is not his plan for us! And while there are many, many misunderstandings out there about what it means to be a woman of God, we can't start with them. No, the problem is bigger than that. In order to untangle the mess and get back to the heart of God's plan, we have to go back to the beginning.

Not to the beginning of our own stories. . . . No, we need to go all the way back to *the* beginning.

THE CREATOR

I have always been fascinated with opening lines. Books, movies, plays, poems, even speeches. No matter the medium, the opening line is one of massive significance. It sets the tone. It creates the mood. It tells the audience a lot about what's going to happen. In fact, I got a little book a long time ago that was simply a compilation of opening lines. I loved it! I loved it so much that, as a teenager, I forced my family to play a game in which I would read a line, and they would have to guess what it was from. They didn't like it as much as I did. In fact, I'm pretty sure they only tolerated it once. But the fact remains, I thought it was awesome! Opening lines are important, and good writers put a lot of thought into where and how to start.

The opening line of Genesis is a perfect example. "In the beginning, God created the heavens and the earth" (Gen. 1:1). It's so simple, so well known (it was in the book—in case you were wondering), yet these simple words convey a ton of meaning. With these words, we find out what the focus of Genesis—of the entire Bible, really—will be: God.

With these first words of Genesis, the Holy Spirit crashes onto the pages of Scripture with a triumphant declaration that this is

God's story. He is the one who creates. He is the focus, the subject, the foundation on which all else depends. He is the beginning; before anything else, he was. He is the main character—not us, not our sin, and certainly not Satan. This is not our story! What we do, what we accomplish (or don't), what man-made standard we live up to, is not the point! We are not center stage, the lights are not focused on us, and that, my friend, is a really good thing. There is so much freedom and so much hope in that truth. And, as we will see, there is so much love.

This is God's story. Every sentence, every moment, is centered on him and him alone. "In the beginning, God . . ." They are little words, but they fill every page of the whole Bible. They flow through every story, gird each chapter, and drape themselves over every second of every day of all time.

As far as opening lines go, this is the best. Not just because it is masterfully written but also because it brings the hope our hearts need and sets the stage for what's to come. It is so easy to skim past it, but it is radical, filled with thunder and power. God is God!

Were we talking about anyone else, this opening line might fill us with dread. But this is the Lord! He is not some authoritarian dictator or narcissistic ruler—this is God who, as we will see, is both loving and love itself. When he created the world, every detail flowed from his abundant love.

THE CONTEXT

Have you ever played around on Google Earth? Maybe started with a view of the earth as a whole and then scrolled in until you were looking at the satellite picture of your home? It's fun to see the big picture so quickly followed by the details.

The creation account in Genesis is written like that. It starts with the super-huge big picture and then moves closer to show us a more detailed view. Moses, under the inspiration of the Spirit of God, does not jump around to show us different things that happened, nor does he give us a bulleted, chronological account. Rather, he zooms in a little at a time, showing us an increasingly detailed picture of the days of creation.

Genesis, which means "beginnings," is the title of the book. It's derived from the first words of verse 1, "In the beginning ... ," and is a fitting title for a book that is about to tell us the beginning of all things! In fact, the verse goes on to say that exact thing: "... God created the heavens and the earth." Verse 1, then, is sort of like a title and subtitle. It's as if Genesis is called *The Book of Beginnings: Wherein God Creates Everything*. Then we get to verse 2, and the creation account kicks off: "The earth was without form and void, and darkness was over the face of the deep. And the Spirit of God was hovering over the face of the waters."

I don't know about you, but Genesis 1:2 has always sort of confused me. At times it's felt out of place or simply didn't make sense to me. But this verse is incredibly important!

First, it focuses our attention on the place of God's creative acts. From the whole of the universe, Genesis 1:2 zooms in on the specific location of Earth itself. "It sets the scene, making the earth our vantage point."[1]

Second, Genesis 1:2 serves as an overview of the creation event. This is not step one of creation. It's not that when God started creating things, he took some primordial goo and began forming it. Not at all. Instead, this verse describes the process of creation. In his commentary on Genesis, John D. Currid wrote, "The universe, and particularly the earth, is now pictured as it appeared in the process of creation."[2] It's a big-picture view of the events that will unfold in greater detail in the verses that follow.

1. Derek Kidner, *Genesis: An Introduction and Commentary* (Downers Grove, IL: InterVarsity Press, 1967), 44.
2. John D. Currid, *Genesis*, vol. 1, *Genesis 1:1–25:18*, Evangelical Press Study Commentary (Darlington, UK: Evangelical Press, 2003), 60.

Third, this verse presents the themes of the creation account. It draws our attention to three things we need to understand for anything else in the creation account to make sense to us: (1) the earth was without form, (2) it was void, and (3) the Spirit of God was hovering.[3]

1. The word for "without form," or formless,[4] carries with it the idea of chaos. Of wildness. It's the picture of a vast, untamed wilderness that God is bringing under control.
2. The word translated "void," or empty,[5] means completely devoid of all living things. In fact, later in the Scriptures (Isa. 34:11; Jer. 4:23), it is used to describe an utterly barren wasteland. It paints a picture of a vast, silent nothingness that God then fills.
3. The word for "hovering" is used later, in Deuteronomy 32:11, to describe a mother bird, her wings spread protectively over her young. It's the beautiful image of the Spirit of God—active and present—stationed over his creation to love and nurture it.

Chaos to order. Empty to full. The loving, personal presence of God. Keep those things in mind as we go on.

In verse 3, Moses moves another step closer, and the details come into focus. Now we get to the actual events of creation! God, by the power of his word alone, calls all things into being. Through this concert of colors, sounds, shapes, and smells, the three key elements bind the creation account together.

With each verse, we see the three points of verse 2 unfold. Derek Kidner put it so well when he said that "God's normal

3. Martin Kessler and Karel Deurloo, *A Commentary on Genesis: The Book of Beginnings* (Mahwah, NJ: Paulist Press, 2004), 16.
4. The Hebrew word *tōhû*.
5. The Hebrew word *bōhû*.

method is to work from the formless to the formed. The whole process is creation. . . . Indeed, the six days now to be described can be viewed as the positive counterpart of the twin negatives 'without form and void', matching them with form and fullness."[6]

God deals with the chaos, the "without form," by bringing order. He creates time, days, nights, stars for charting seasons and paths. He separates the land and the seas. He gives everything a place and a name. He brings order because our God is a God who delights in order; he cares for his creation, and every part of it has a place.

But God doesn't just bring order to the chaos in creation; he also deals with the emptiness, the "void." He fills the earth with every form of life. Creatures of all sizes and shapes emerge at his call. Plants grow and flourish. His creativity overflows into the brightest blues and pinks, the richest scents of flowers, the chest-rattling boom of thunder, and the soul-lifting silence that comes after a rain.

And through each moment of creation, the Spirit of God is present, active, personal, and loving. When Moses gives us the three themes of the creation account, he isn't just helping us to see the pattern of creation (filling and ordering)—he is also showing us God's heart toward his creation. God is a personal, loving God.

The days of creation form a grand symphony. Each moment adds new instruments as the music builds. With each beat, we see "And God said . . . ," and something amazing appears, and ". . . it was good." The pattern repeats over and over again but with growing complexity and beauty. The great conductor draws in each player, and the air fills with the rising sounds of nature's worship. As the music swells, we know that the best is about to come. We sit in edge-of-our-seat expectation. And God said. And it happened. And it was good!

But—

6. Kidner, *Genesis*, 45–46.

But suddenly the conductor stops.

The interruption in Genesis 1:26 is, in itself, dramatic. The silence is deafening. "Why would you stop?" our hearts cry out. Did something go wrong? But the conductor isn't upset. No, like a giddy new dad showing off home videos, he turns to the audience and says, "Get ready—this is the best part!"

THE TRIUNE GOD

Each member of the Trinity—the Father, the Son, and the Holy Spirit—has been present in creation, but here they stop, invite us in, and discuss what they will do next: "Let us make man" (Gen. 1:26).

To be honest, many of us often breeze past the fact that all three members of the Trinity speak in communion with one another. But it is so important because here, in the opening verses of Scripture, we see that God is Trinitarian, and knowing he's Trinitarian changes the way we see what has just happened in creation, what he's about to do, and what it means for us to live as his people in the world. We saw that he was loving in the way he created and cared for his creation, but now we see that love is a foundational aspect of who he is. Love is what prompted him to create in the first place.

To see that, however, we need to quickly clarify a few things about this idea of "Trinity." Let's start with the fact that the word *Trinity* isn't even used in the Bible. It's a word that was used years later to encapsulate the progressive revelation of the whole Bible's teaching of who God is.[7] But the problem is, words are seldom simple or clear, especially when they need to distill something as huge and complicated as the Trinitarian nature of God! Because of that, we need to hit on a couple of points to make sure we're all on the same page.

---

7. John H. Leith, *Basic Christian Doctrine* (Louisville: Westminster/John Knox Press, 1993), 46.

First, God exists as the Trinity. He is not *like* a trinity or *in* a trinity—he *is* the Trinity.[8] In saying that he is the Trinity, we are saying that the Father, the Son, and the Spirit are one God, three persons. Not three different modes of being, or three different gods working together—not at all.[9] The Father, the Son, and the Holy Spirit are of one substance (or nature) while at the same time three distinct, unmingled persons.

Second, while each member of the Trinity performs different functions throughout Scripture, it is also equally true that all three members participate in every action.[10] We cannot, and should not, try to sharply separate what they do. We see this more clearly when we read about the life of Christ in the New Testament: the Father sent the Son, the Son lived and died in our place, and the Spirit revealed him to us. All three persons of the Trinity worked together to accomplish redemption. And that's the same premise at work in the early verses of Genesis. The Father, the Son, and the Holy Spirit all work together in creation. Without announcing that God is three persons, Genesis 1 shows all three present and active.

Finally, the names we have for the members of the Trinity—Father, Son, and Spirit—in no way imply, or should be taken to mean, that there is a power hierarchy between the members of the Godhead. All three persons are absolutely equal, and there is no natural subordination between them.[11]

God is Trinitarian. The question, then—as I'm sure you're wondering—is, why is that fact important in verse 26? Why does

8. "The Eleventh Council of Toledo on the Trinity," in *The Christian Theology Reader,* 2nd ed., ed. Alister E. McGrath (Malden, MA: Blackwell Publishers, 2001), 201.

9. Leith, *Basic Christian Doctrine,* 49.

10. Leith, 50.

11. John H. Gerstner, Douglas F. Kelly, and Philip Rollinson, *The Westminster Confession of Faith Commentary* (Signal Mountain, TN: Summertown Texts, 1992), 28.

it matter that God declares himself to be Trinitarian in the same sentence that he declares he's going to make people?

THE OVERFLOWING LOVE

When God speaks in Genesis 1:26 and says, "Let us . . . ," he speaks as the Trinitarian God: the Father, the Son, and the Spirit existing in perfect relationship within himself. This means that relationship is a huge part of the nature of God; he has existed, and does exist, and always will exist in relationship. Moreover, he dwells in relationship perfectly, because he is God and he is perfect. There is perfect unity among the Father, the Son, and the Spirit: no vying for power or position, no loneliness, and no lack. That little word *us* declares that God is Trinitarian and dwells in perfect loving relationship. This brings us to the next point we need to see: God doesn't need us.[12]

Can we sit with that for a second?

We are not needed! If God the Father were without the Son or Spirit, we could say that maybe he was lonely. Maybe he created us because he needed a friend? Or perhaps he longed for creatures to worship him or stroke his ego? He is God, after all. But because God exists in perfect relationship within himself, none of that is true. God doesn't need us. In fact, because we know from elsewhere in Scripture that God is love,[13] we know that he *must* exist as a trinity because perfect love cannot exist on its own; it must have both someone to love and someone to share that love with.[14] God isn't lonely!

12. Gerstner, Kelly, and Rollinson, 27.

13. "So we have come to know and to believe the love that God has for us. God is love, and whoever abides in love abides in God, and God abides in him" (1 John 4:16).

14. "Richard of St Victor on Love within the Trinity," in *The Christian Theology Reader*, 2nd ed., ed. Alister E. McGrath (Malden, MA: Blackwell

He doesn't get lonely, he doesn't need someone to hang out with, and he didn't create us to fill some lack that he had; God is perfectly satisfied within himself. So when God calls us into his presence in verse 26 and says, "Let us create man," we can know with absolute certainty that it is not *need* that prompts his actions—it is *want*.[15] He creates out of his own free will, motivated by his overflowing love. He didn't need to create us, but he chose to; it wasn't lack that prompted him but abundance.

The perfect love that exists within God himself, that drives and connects him, overflowed in abundance, and he chose to create beings on which to lavish that love, because perfect love is always outward focused. That abundance—that overflowing, outward-facing love—led him to create you. He wanted you. He isn't a lonely being, longing for someone to love him back. He isn't manipulative, twisting our affections to fill some emotional void. He is the King, perfectly sufficient in himself but exceedingly generous and with love abounding.

God didn't create you because he needed you to do something for him. He doesn't have a to-do list of errands he needs someone to run or a bunch of tasks to be accomplished. He has no lack for you to fill. He doesn't need you, but he wanted you. Do you feel the love in that?

That night as I left my daughter's room and listened to the blankets rustling softly as she settled down to sleep, I was reminded of this great love. A love that is so much bigger and better than mine. I love my children, and I can sit in their rooms at night and whisper words of hope and remind them that my love is unconditional, but I also know deep in my heart that I can't fulfill that promise or keep those words—at least, not on my own. The

Publishers, 2001), 204.

15. Arthur W. Pink, *The Attributes of God* (Grand Rapids: Baker Book House, 1975), 9–10.

day will come, possibly even the very next day, when my selfishness and their actions will collide. There will be times when I will allow my hurts or fears or longings to twist my reactions, and I will, I know, allow their actions to influence the way in which I love them. I will be tempted to hold their choices against them and make them earn my love back. And while I wish my love were unconditional, I know that sin prevents that. To love my kids—or anyone, for that matter—well, I must cling to the source of love, to the One who is love.

But God's love isn't like mine. His overflowing love prompted him to create humans, and, as we will see, his specific love moved heaven and earth to bring us back when everything went wrong. His love truly is abundant, full, and all-encompassing. It is not something you can earn by doing all the right things or by being the woman you think you're supposed to be. And in Christ, it's not something you can lose by failing to live up to whatever standard you think there is. It is perfect because he is perfect.

In Genesis 1:26, God declares that he's going to make people, and in saying that, he declares that he's going to make them out of his abundant love. But he doesn't stop there! In addition to both of those truths, he declares that he is going to make them for a *reason*. He is going to create image bearers. Creatures made in his image to be like him. Creatures who could exist in loving, personal relationship with him. Creatures he could pour his abundant love upon. Creatures who would image him by bringing that outward-facing love into the world and bringing flourishing in his name.

In the following chapters, we will look at what it means to be made in his image and how we are called to live out our image bearing. But as we do, hold on to this truth: you were created out of the abundance of God's perfect love. The ways in which we are invited to live that out are gifts of love from him meant to bring us flourishing. We do not live as image bearers to earn God's love, nor do we obey out of fear of losing it. In other words, his love, not our actions, is the foundation. We are image bearers, we are children of God, and we are deeply, powerfully loved.

SCRIPTURE TO CONSIDER

Genesis 1:1–26
Deuteronomy 32:10–11
Psalm 33
Ephesians 3:14–19

FOR REFLECTION

1. Describe a time when you felt like you could earn more of God's love. What are some things that you have done or seen other people do to earn his favor?
2. Describe a time you worried that you could lose God's love. How did that affect the way you interacted with him?
3. God's presence is an aspect of creation that will grow increasingly important as we move forward. Read Deuteronomy 32:10–11. How does the picture presented here, combined with what we saw in Genesis 1:2, illustrate the presence of God? What does it tell us about his disposition toward his creation?
4. Write a list of words or ideas that come to mind when you think about the love of God.
5. God didn't need to create us, but he wanted to; he was motivated by love. How does this understanding of his love change the way we relate to him? How would your life change right now if you truly believed that you couldn't earn more or lose any of God's love?

2

THE IMAGE WE BEAR

"Let us make man in our image, after our likeness." (Gen. 1:26)

I don't have an accent. I mean, I don't think I have one. I guess if you insist that everyone has some sort of accent, then you could classify mine as "American Broadcast," which is just another way of saying generic American—the type you hear on the radio. I don't really have an accent—until I get up in front of a room to speak. When I'm standing on stage to teach, a Southern drawl slips off my tongue, complete with all the y'all's and twang you'd expect of a girl born and bred in the South. Except I wasn't born in the South—I'm from northern Virginia, which, if you ask any northern Virginian, is not in the South; it's in the North. But no matter where in the country I am, if I am speaking in front of an audience, I will probably have a Southern accent.

I don't know why it happens. Possibly it's a weird nervous habit. More likely, however, it's because I went to school in the South, so many of the teachers who influenced me the most throughout my life were Southern. Without even meaning for it to happen, their accents rubbed off on me, and now, unless I try very hard to prevent it, I will, without fail, vocally mimic all those teachers when I am standing on stage to teach.

And while we're talking about it, this whole vocal-mimic thing doesn't just happen when I'm teaching. If I'm around people from a different part of the world or with a different accent, I inevitably start mimicking their pronunciations and inflections. If I've been watching a TV show with characters from another place or even if I'm reading a book in which the characters have accents, I will start speaking like them. I can't help it; it just happens. I am, for whatever reason, a mimic when it comes to voices. I'm not trying to do it. It's just that my brain and my voice sometimes don't consult me.

It's a weird quirk and one that I try to be aware of, because I don't want to ever offend someone or have them think I'm mocking them. It's just that the more I am around someone, the more I pick up their mannerisms and pronunciations and the more I find I imitate them. And you know, that's true for all of us.

The old adage "We become what we behold" is true, and it's true in all areas of our lives. Without meaning or even trying to, we pick up the habits, mannerisms, behaviors, ideas, even thought patterns of the people who surround us. We are all, in one way or another, mimics. And that's not a bad thing. In fact, it's part of who we were created to be.

CREATED TO BE GOD'S IMAGE BEARERS

Genesis 1 opens with God creating everything. We see him fling planets into orbit, call forth the oceans and mountains, craft the biggest elephants and the tiniest insects. In every instance, we see a pattern of "And God said . . . ," then something is created, ". . . and it was good." But then we get to verse 26, and the pattern changes. Here we are given a behind-the-scenes look into what is about to happen, and rather than just doing what he's going to do, God invites us in and tells us his plan.

That's huge! Every other time thus far, God simply acts. But not here. Here he stops and, with excitement, declares that he is going to do something magnificent; he is going to create humanity: "Let us make man in our image, after our likeness."

In the last chapter, we looked at the first part of that verse, "Let us . . . ," and at how God was motivated by his abundant, outward-focused love. But the verse goes on, and the triune God—Father, Son, and Holy Spirit—declares that he is going to make people and he's going to create them for a very specific purpose: to bear his image. Humans will be different from everything else, above everything else, because of this purpose.

Purpose is an important thing. It propels us, gives our lives meaning, and shapes our decisions and actions. Without one, we wander. With the wrong one, we wither. We need a purpose, and we were created with an amazing one! But when we don't understand what that is, when we don't know that God's primary plan for us is to be his image, or when we don't understand what that means, we will start to look for meaning elsewhere. We'll make purposes out of our careers, our families, or our hobbies. Our personalities, our relationships, and our choices will start to become the forces that give our lives direction. We'll even look to people in the Bible and start thinking that our purpose is to be like them. That's how we end up in situations in which we're studying women like Ruth or Hannah and, rather than seeing them as women whom God used in his story of redemption, we start to see them as nothing more than elevated checklists of what we must do to become real women of God.

Jobs and families and women of worth from the Bible are important and good, but they are not our *purpose*; they are not what gives our lives meaning. And when we make them our purpose, things start to get muddled. It's like trying to read a book in the dark—it just doesn't work. We need the truth of God's purpose for us, the truth of what it means to be made in his image, to shine a light on our hearts. Not just to show us who he created us to be but to allow us to put all those other things back in their correct place as well.

Genesis 1:26 is a little verse, but it has huge implications for our lives.

For so long I bought into the lie that my purpose was to simply be a good Christian woman and do all the right things. I believed that the highest aim of womanhood was to be a wife and a mother, and if I couldn't do that, I was supposed to do everything else. I didn't understand that God's purpose for me was not about that at all. His purpose for me was not about what I could do—in fact, it wasn't even about *me*. It was about him!

We can "glorify God and enjoy him forever"[1] because we are his image bearers. We can be in a relationship with him because we are his image. We have dignity and worth and value because we alone in all creation are his images. Everything we are and everything we are called to be radiates from this one truth. It all starts here.

How have we so easily overlooked or misunderstood the heart of who God created us to be? Perhaps it's because Genesis 1:26 is just one little verse. Or maybe because it feels like we should just get it without having to think too hard. Or maybe because it's something that we've heard in passing so often. Whatever the reason, many of us don't really understand what God is saying and why it matters as much as it does.

But when we breeze past this verse, this declaration, we are missing the foundational point of God's plan. Everyone's heart whispers questions like "What's God's plan for me?" or "Who did God create me to be?" They are insistent, important questions. Questions that demand an answer. But if we're not looking to God to answer them, we'll look to something else—and nothing else can satisfy. It's like a puzzle with a missing piece. You can grab a pair of scissors and trim some cardboard and hope the

---

1. The Westminster Shorter Catechism, answer 1.

substitute will fit, and it might, but it's not the same, and the finished picture won't shine with its intended beauty. The truth is, much of the exhaustion, the striving, and the shame-filled visions of Christianity radiate from this point.

To be clear, I'm not saying we're trying to miss God's plan for us. I'm simply saying that if you feel overwhelmed with all the things you're "supposed" to do as a woman of God, if you're exhausted and burned out and a little bit lost, then maybe this is a point of confusion in your life too. It absolutely was for me.

As we will see, understanding this point affects the way we view ourselves and the way we see others. It affects the way we read his Word and our relationship with him. It changes the way we see singleness, marriage, and motherhood, the way we do ministry. Even the way we worship is impacted by understanding what it means to be made in the image of God.

WHAT'S IN A WORD?

What, then, does it mean? Words are important. They have meaning and carry weight depending on how and where they are used. When God said, "Let us make man in our image, after our likeness," those words are no different. They have meaning—a real, actual definition that impacts how we understand what is being said. So, let's start here, with the two words God uses to describe how he is going to make humans: *image* and *likeness*.

Image

"Image" is the Hebrew noun ṣĕlĕm. It originally meant "something cut off."[2] It carries the idea of a carving, a sculpture, or a work of art—anything crafted to look like something else. Often

2. Ernest Klein, *A Comprehensive Etymological Dictionary of the Hebrew Language* (New York: Macmillan, 1987), 548.

in the Old Testament, the word is used to refer to idols—physical representations of deities crafted to be worshiped in place of the actual being. They were objects made to resemble and stand in place of something else.[3]

In the Bible, the word *image* is used to refer to a physical object crafted to look like and to represent the original. "In our image," then, communicates the idea that we resemble God in a very real, concrete, and visible way. God is the original, and we were cut off, carved, in such a way as to mirror him. We see this idea again just a few chapters later when Adam has a son "in his own likeness, after his image" (Gen. 5:3). Adam's son looked like him—there was a resemblance.

Therefore, the idea of "image" is, at least in part, a visible thing. To be clear, this doesn't mean it is *only* visible or physical, but the word used here clearly indicates that it's at least *in part* visible. Something about our physical presence displays God to the world around us.[4] I love the way George C. Hammond put it. He said we are a "visible representation of the invisible God."[5] How beautiful is that? Far from the notion that the image of God is just spiritual or internal, the word *image* indicates that we, in our physical bodies, represent God to creation.[6] And I know that can feel uncomfortable and, for many of us, is far from what we thought to be the case. But in a world in which we swing wildly between overly spiritualizing or overly objectifying our bodies, getting this right is so important. Our bodies matter to God.

3. Keep in mind, the idols created were not the actual gods; they had no power in themselves. They were simply statues that represented what the people were trying to worship.

4. Jerram Barrs, *Through His Eyes: God's Perspective on Women in the Bible* (Wheaton, IL: Crossway, 2009), 16.

5. George C. Hammond, *It Has Not Yet Appeared What We Shall Be: A Reconsideration of the Imago Dei in Light of Those with Severe Cognitive Disabilities* (Phillipsburg, NJ: P&R Publishing, 2017), 138.

6. Hammond, 73.

What's more, while God the Father is spirit (see John 4:24) and does not have a physical body, Christ was "the image of the invisible God" (Col. 1:15) and is "the radiance of the glory of God and the exact imprint of his nature" (Heb. 1:3). Jesus is the fullness of the image of God. When Christ came to earth, he wasn't made to look like us—we were already patterned after him.[7]

Our bodies display something about God. I can't pretend to know all that entails, but I do know this: your whole self, including your body, is important. We cannot separate the importance of our physical selves from our spiritual selves; they are divinely entwined. As Gerhard von Rad said, "Therefore, one will do well to split the physical from the spiritual as little as possible: the whole man is created in the image of God."[8]

Likeness

But what's being described here is more than just physical. The other word that God used in this passage is the word *likeness*.[9] *Likeness* is also a noun that deals with something being of like manner or comparing two things and finding them to be similar. When combined with "after our," it becomes an explanatory prepositional phrase. This means that the phrase "after our likeness" isn't a new way in which we image God; instead, it helps to further explain what had already been said.[10] It's a clarifying

7. "Christ has always been God's image, from before the creation of humanity. . . . In other words, God knew that standard for what humanity was to be—the humanity of Christ—before creating Adam/*adam*. . . . God created humanity at the outset in the image of God, in harmony with Christ as God's image." John F. Kilner, *Dignity and Destiny: Humanity in the Image of God* (Grand Rapids: Eerdmans, 2015), 80–81.

8. Gerhard von Rad, *Genesis: A Commentary*, rev. ed. (Philadelphia: Westminster Press, 1972), 58.

9. The Hebrew word used here is *dĕmuwth*.

10. John D. Currid, *Genesis*, vol. 1, *Genesis 1:1–25:18*, Evangelical Press Study Commentary (Darlington, UK: Evangelical Press, 2003), 85.

phrase. It takes that word *image* and opens it up to include all the ways in which we are like God. It helps to solidify in our minds that, as image bearers, our whole self is made like him.

To be clear, this is not a situation where two words are used to talk about two different aspects of ourselves. For example, *image* is not referring to our bodies and *likeness* to our hearts or vice versa. Nor is it a case of the same word being repeated for emphasis. Instead, this is an explanation, a building upon what was already said; the words are linked.

Likeness opens up the idea that we are like God in many ways, not just physically but emotionally, intellectually, and spiritually as well. It can then be rightly said that in any way we are like God, we bear his image. *Likeness* confirms that the *whole person* is made in the image of God without distinction and that *all people* are image bearers without distinction.[11] We were fully crafted in such a way as to bear God's image, and that is an amazing, awe-inspiring, life-giving thing!

It's also important to note that while we are like God in many ways, those ways do not make up, or constitute, the image of God in us. Rather, we can do those things because we were made in God's image.[12] Our functions do not make up the image of God in us; we simply are God's images because he has declared us to be. This is important because it clarifies that no one is more the image of God than anyone else and all people, regardless of their physical or cognitive abilities, are image bearers. All people matter.

Being made in God's image and likeness means that every part of you (internally and externally) is important to him. And while the things we do matter, those things do not give us worth.

11. D. J. A. Clines, "The Image of God in Man," *Tyndale Bulletin* 19 (1968): 101.

12. Hammond, *It Has Not Yet Appeared*, 168.

Our value, our dignity, is not found in what we do; it is found in the image we bear. Before we did anything, before we earned it in any way, apart from any abilities or actions, God created us as his images on the earth. We have value and worth, not because of what we can bring and contribute but simply because God has declared that we alone are his images. You, my friend, matter to the God of the universe!

Unique

Before we continue, we need to take a look at one other word used in Genesis 1:26. It's the word *man*. The Hebrew word is *adam*, which is a generic word meaning "mankind."[13] When God declares that he will create image bearers, he says he will make them in the form of humans—not just a single man but men and women. This is confirmed when God carries out his plan and creates "man in his image, in the image of God he created him; male and female he created them" (Gen. 1:27). God's plan, from the very beginning, is to create both men and women in his image.

Some Bible versions even translate *adam* as "mankind" in verse 26, as a way to help us to understand that God always planned on making both Adam and Eve.[14] Eve was not an afterthought, as we'll see in chapter 5. But while I love that translators are trying to clarify this, it does carry one small problem. It's easy to see "mankind" and think that God placed his image

13. Currid, *Genesis*, 111.

14. Throughout the creation account, Eve is simply referred to as "the woman"; she does not receive her name until 3:20 when Adam names her "Eve." And while there is significance to that, as we'll see toward the end of this book, for consistency's sake and to convey the agency that she had as a created being and an image bearer, I have opted to use her name throughout this book, even when dealing with passages pre-naming. Names are important; they humanize us and allow for a personal connection, even through writing, that you cannot get with a descriptor.

on humanity as a collective unit—that we are all partial image bearers who only fully display his image when we are joined with others. But that is not what God says.

When God declares that he will place his image on the earth in the form of humans, he declares that he will make unique individuals who will each bear his image fully and yet differently.[15]

It can be easy for me to miss this fact. To think that, somehow, God's image is not complete in me and needs a man or a marriage to round it out. But that's not true. God places his image on the earth in the form of men and women. We all bear God's image, though we all bear it uniquely.

Living out the image of God is meant to be done in community, as we will see in more detail later. The outward-focused love that prompted him to create us is displayed in the way we live both for and with others. In other words, something amazing and beautiful and divinely radiant happens when we join together. We display God's image in a new and powerful way when that happens, whether in marriage or in ministry or in friendships. But do not lose sight of the fact that it is already present in you; we are, each of us, unique image bearers of God.

WHAT IMAGES ARE

Mirrors

I live, I am convinced, in one of the most beautiful places in the entire world: the foothills of the Blue Ridge Mountains. At almost any point throughout my day, especially if I'm out running errands, I can look up and see their blue-gray silhouette standing proudly in the distance. But one of my favorite places isn't on the mountains—it's under them.

Hidden beneath the rolling hills and the tree-covered Blue

15. Barrs, *Through His Eyes*, 18.

Ridges are ancient and gigantic caverns. I have visited them countless times and never cease to be amazed by their beauty. After waiting in line in the humid Virginia heat, you eventually descend a set of stairs that have been cut into the rock. As you do, the lights shift from the glaring summer sun to the dim golden glow of wire-caged lights, the air gets cooler on your cheeks, and the voices of those around you naturally shift to a gentle, awe-filled whisper.

The tour takes you through amazing caverns. You see massive rock formations and huge open spaces, and then you get to my favorite spot. Dream Lake looks like a huge cave filled with stalactites and stalagmites that seems to stretch out as far and as deep as your eyes can see. As you try to take it all in, however, your tour guide will explain that what you are looking at isn't a giant cavern at all, but a small underground lake. The water of the lake is so still that it reflects the cave ceiling perfectly, creating a mirror image indistinguishable from the real thing. What looks like a massive cavern is actually a puddle less than two feet deep. It's an image. A mirror. A reflection.

Mirrors are common in our world. Some do their job well, like Dream Lake, which reflects perfectly. Others, not so well, like the mirror in the dressing room that convinced me that those jeans were worth the price. But whether they image perfectly or distort dramatically, mirrors all serve one purpose. They reflect. They don't have to work at this; they simply do it because they are mirrors.

We have been looking at the words God used to describe his creation of humanity: men and women would be both his image and his likeness. And we've looked in detail at the literal meaning of those words. But now we need to turn our attention to what that actually means, what God was communicating when he used them. We know now that we were created to be like God somehow and that every part of us, both internal and external, matters to him. But what does it look like to be made in his image? In other words, at a very basic level, what do images do?

Like mirrors, image bearers reflect the very image of God. He created us to reflect him just as he created Dream Lake to reflect the cavern ceiling. And because we were made in his image *and* likeness, our whole selves reflect him; we look like him physically, emotionally, spiritually, relationally, morally, and so on.[16] What this means is that our existence shouts of the existence of God. The intricacies of our bodies, our anatomy and physiology, declare the wonders of his creative nature. The depth of our emotions, even the very way we think and relate to one another, the way we love, was designed to reflect his character. And by reflecting, we direct attention back to him.

When I take my daughter shopping and we stand in the dressing room together while she shows me the dress she's hoping we'll buy and I look at her in the mirror, my heart doesn't swell with love for that reflection. I know it's just a reflection. Rather, my heart is overwhelmed by love for my daughter—her twirling reflection just draws my attention back to her. It's the same thing that was designed to happen here. We, as images of God, were designed to point others back to him. When people see us, or anyone else for that matter, they get a glimpse of God because we were created as his image and images reflect.

Do we reflect him perfectly? No, sin has gotten in the way (and we'll get to that), but we were still created to display him and to reflect him to the world around us.

Similarly, in ancient times, rulers would erect statues of themselves in the farthest corners of their empires. Although not mirrors, these statues reminded the people who their ruler was by reflecting his likeness for all to see. It continually showed them who they served, who they paid their taxes to, who protected

16. Kilner, *Dignity and Destiny*, 114–15.

them; in a very real sense, it reminded them who they belonged to. These images, like the images of a king stamped onto a coin, were marks of ownership and symbols of allegiance. In the same way, when God declared that we would bear his image, he declared that the whole earth was his, that we serve him. Like statues in a far-off land, we are images that declare God as ruler of all.

Imitators

We were created to be the image of God. That means that all people everywhere throughout all of time and history have dignity, worth, and value because they bear God's image. We cannot earn that, we cannot lose that. It's simply how God created us out of his abundant love. But as much as I love the analogies we've been looking at, we are more than statues or mirrors. They are static objects, but we are living, breathing agents of God's design. And while we are mirrors that reflect the image of God simply by existing, the full expression of that image comes from how we live it out.[17] We are mimics. We are imitators.

They say that imitation is the purest form of flattery, but it's more than that. It's our *purpose*. We were created to look like God in all ways, not just on the outside but on the inside too. What's more, we were designed to act like him as well. Imitation is the idea that girds all these others together; it runs through them and connects them in a purposeful way.

Imitation is more than just acting like God, though. It includes our motivations as well. God designed us to think like he does, love like he does, feel like he does. This is why image bearing is foundational to all we are. Every time Scripture tells us to do what God does, it echoes back to who God created us to be. Every rule, every instruction, every command, and every calling is anchored in this idea that we were designed to imitate God

17. Clines, "Image of God in Man," 101.

and, in doing so, image him to the world. This idea of imitating God is the basis for our very identities. It informs our decisions; it focuses our motivations. It means that everything we do, ever, should reflect his character. And being made in his image is what allows us to imitate him in the first place.[18]

Imitation is sewn into the very fiber of our being. We don't have to work at it—it's simply what we are. We imitate whatever we have drawn closest to, because God created us to be natural mimics who, without even trying, become what we behold.

DRAW NEAR

Apart from anything we do, apart from anything we contribute or bring to the table, we are images of God. To be clear, our ability to think or love or be in relationships, and so on, do not constitute the image of God in us; they are not what the image *is*. We can do those things *because* God made us in his image; he made us like him. We have been given honor and value and worth and dignity because we are all made in God's image. What this means is that our value and our purpose are not dependent on us or our abilities; it's all about him.

If we are left to our own devices, this is an overwhelming and even terrifying truth. How can we bear the weight of this responsibility? But image bearing is not supposed to be a burden. Instead, it is an invitation to draw near, to stand close, and to let God transform us from the inside out. Mirrors don't have to work at being mirrors—they just are. Likewise, we don't have to strive to be images; we simply have to draw near to God to make sure that what we are reflecting is what we were designed to reflect in the first place. He is going to do the work through us. Is there an

---

18. G. K. Beale, *A New Testament Biblical Theology: The Unfolding of the Old Testament in the New* (Grand Rapids: Baker Academic, 2011), 30.

aspect of obedience in how we live this out? Absolutely, and we'll get into that more later. But for now, know that being an image bearer is not about what you do; it's about who he is. We are being invited to rest in his presence because something beautiful happens when we spend our time near our Father. We start to think like him. We start to live like him. We start to look like him. We're imitators; it's what we do!

Being an image bearer is the heart of our purpose as humans. It is the foundation for who we are and who God created us to be. Before we were daughters, friends, wives, or mothers, we were declared image bearers. This status does not depend on your gender, the color of your skin, or if you have any children at all. Dear friend, you are an image bearer, and that means your life has meaning and value and purpose.

When God said, "Let us make man in our image, after our likeness . . . ," he was declaring that he would create us out of his abundant, overflowing, outward-focused love. But he was also declaring that we, as those made in his image and likeness, would be imitators of him. Like mirrors we would reflect him to the world, like statues we would declare his authority over our lives, and like imitators we would mimic the character of God. In the following chapters, we will look at the foundational ways God calls us to live out his image on the earth, but before we get there we need to understand that everything that will follow is anchored here. Being made in the image of God is the heart of who we are—it is our very purpose.

We are image bearers; we are imitators. So, draw near to God. Push your way through the crowd if you have to. Close your computer; set down your phone if it helps. Drown out the voices that tell you that you need to do more or look different, the shame that says you're not enough or the comparison that screams you're way too much. Just come and sit with him. Read his Word, not as a task to check off your list, but as a way to get to know this God who loves you so deeply. Rest in the truth that you were created to look like, to be like, and to represent the God of the universe. That is your purpose. And it's not about what you do—it's about who you already are.

SCRIPTURE TO CONSIDER

Genesis 1:1–26
Matthew 22:15–22
Colossians 1:15–20

FOR REFLECTION

1. Describe a time in your life when you started to act like the people you were around. What was it like? How did it make you feel? How have you seen this happen in the people around you?

2. Before reading this chapter, what would you have said your purpose in life was? How did that impact the choices you've made or the things you've done? As humans, we're very good at coming up with purposes for ourselves. What are some things you have seen other people make their purpose?

3. The words *image* and *likeness* teach that our whole selves matter: our bodies, minds, hearts, emotions . . . everything. Is that something you've struggled with in the past? It's easy to rate the parts of ourselves in order of importance. Take a moment to write out a list of how you have rated the parts of you in the past. Does this understanding of image and likeness change your list?

4. Image bearing is about reflecting God to the world around us. Doing that, however, requires that we draw near to him so that what we're imitating is the One we were created to

imitate in the first place. What does it look like for a person to draw near to God? What does it look like in your life?

5. Jesus Christ is the fullness of the image of God. How does seeing ourselves as patterned after him impact the way you think about his life and death on earth? Does it change the way you see him? Yourself?

3

THE CALL TO CREATE

And God blessed them. And God said to them,
"Be fruitful and multiply and fill the earth . . ." (Gen. 1:28)

Legos are a big part of life in my house. They fill toy boxes, line bookshelves, and yes, litter my floors. All my kids love them, but they love them in different ways. One of my children builds each set perfectly and then leaves it assembled to be admired or played with at will. She's not too bothered if they fall apart; the pieces just get absorbed into her play, and, more often than not, she uses them for other games anyway. Another child invents long, complicated stories that last for days and cover every spare inch of the room. She begrudgingly abides by my "there has to be a path for me to get from the door to your bed without hurting myself" rule, but otherwise the story is of utmost importance and every piece has a role to play in her epic adventure.

And then there is my scavenger, my Lego fanatic who would gladly spend every moment of his life with them. He builds the sets, sure, but in a few short days, pieces start disappearing from their assigned space and reappearing as parts of his latest creation. This is my child whose room looks like a Lego bomb exploded, who has walked on Legos for so long that his feet are no longer

49

bothered by them. Who, when given the choice between a picture book and a Lego instruction manual, will choose the instructions as a bedtime book every time.

He loves his Legos, and he loves studying those brightly colored manuals, not just to see how to build things but to see all the different uses for each and every piece. It's one of the beautiful things about Legos, you know, that each piece can be used in a multitude of ways. And while I think of those instruction booklets as teaching me how to build, he looks at them as teaching him how to think. The instructions are imagination-stirring invitations to create. And that, I think, is a pretty amazing type of invitation.

I opened this book by telling you about a moment when all the things I thought I was supposed to be, do, say, and think to qualify as a "real" woman of God crashed down around me and I sat on my bed and wept. I was exhausted and burned out and had no idea who it was that God had created me to be. I had no idea that God's plan for me was bigger and better and more freeing than I had dared to imagine.

That day, after drying my tears, I did something I had never really done before: I opened my Bible and tried to see for myself what God was calling me to. To be honest, not a lot changed that day. But I sought out godly teachers, and, over time, I started to see the beauty and the depth of what it means to be made in the image of God. My life changed when I realized that being an image bearer is the very heart of my purpose. Knowing that it was God's abundant love that prompted him to create us, seeing that he made us with a high purpose, started to transform my heart.

For a time, I simply basked in that. God loves me, and I am an image bearer! Apart from anything I do or anything I contribute, I matter. Can you feel the hope and the peace in that? Soon, however, the all-important question came knocking at my door. . . . Yes, but how? How could I—sinful, broken me—be an image bearer?

What was that supposed to look like in real life? If images reflect and imitate, how do I live that out?

Thankfully God doesn't leave us hanging. In Genesis 1:26, he declares what he is about to do and why: make humans to be his image. In verse 27, he does it: he creates the man and the woman. But God doesn't create them both, call them his image bearers, bestow honor above all creation on them, and then send them away to figure out how to live out their purpose on their own. Not at all! Instead, he gives them instructions. He gives them a plan—a plan that, like Lego instruction books, gives us a pattern and then invites us to go out and create.

"And God blessed them. And God said to them, 'Be fruitful and multiply and fill the earth and subdue it, and have dominion'" (Gen. 1:28). It's called the cultural mandate; it's God's foundational instructions to humanity.

Be fruitful. Multiply. And fill. This, my friend, is where things start to get messy.[1]

A MISTAKEN *MULTIPLY*

When I was a child, being a mom was at the top of all my "what do you want to be when you grow up?" lists. Not only was my mom a mom, but she was the coolest woman I knew. It seemed like the best job ever. I wanted to be a mom more than almost anything in the world.

As I grew up, however, that want became overshadowed by expectation. I started to get the distinct sense that because I was a

1. I know that, for some of you, Genesis 1:28 has been used as a judge's gavel. Or a whip. For many of you there might be weighty, even painful baggage associated with it. I want you to know that I'm with you. While many have used this passage to hurt, God intended it to heal. This passage is filled with hope and life, and if you venture forward with me, you will see that God's love for us overflows in his plan for us to live out our status as bearers of his image.

girl, being a mother was what I was supposed to do. I don't mean *do* as in "do the dishes," something to check off a list. No, in my mind, having a baby was a requirement. It was more than something women did; it was part of what *actually made them women*. I suspect I'm not alone.

Genesis 1:28 starts with a stunning statement: "And God blessed them." The idea of blessing here implies not just a gift but a function as well.[2] It's God turning his face to his children in self-giving.[3] Not only that, but the giving of the blessing carries with it the promise that God himself will enable them to do whatever it is that he is asking them to do.[4] Thus, while we call the cultural mandate a command, a mandate, or even an invitation, the reality is that it is at its heart a blessing. God is blessing his image bearers and calling them to join him in the process of spreading his glory throughout the whole earth. And while it is one single command, it is made up of two distinct parts, or two ways in which we are to live as his images. The second part is the command to subdue and have dominion over the earth, and we'll look at that in the next chapter. But the first is the call to be fruitful, multiply, and fill, and it is here that so much of my confusion rested.

Over and over again, I heard talks or read books where God's command to Adam and Eve to be fruitful and multiply was mentioned and procreation was specifically stated or heavily implied. My longing for a child of my own grew (a perfectly fine thing), as did my ingrained belief that having one would take me one step closer to being a real woman of God (not good).

Now, let me be clear: the desire to have children is not wrong,

2. Derek Kidner, *Genesis: An Introduction and Commentary* (Downers Grove, IL: InterVarsity Press, 1967), 52.

3. Kidner, 52.

4. Gordon J. Wenham, *Genesis 1–15*, Word Biblical Commentary 1 (Waco, TX: Word Books, 1987), 33.

or bad, or anything like that. It is a beautiful desire that God has given to many women (though not all, and that's OK too). However, the belief that having a baby is the highest calling of womanhood, that becoming pregnant somehow makes someone a better Christian woman, that motherhood earns a woman status before God or is a woman's whole purpose, was wrong. One hundred percent, completely wrong.

When we wrap up our purpose as women with our ability to have children, we inadvertently cause problems. And not just little problems—we're talking life-shattering problems, heart-wounding problems. This misunderstanding has massive repercussions.

THE WALKING WOUNDED

You may not have experience with this misunderstanding. But the more women I talk with, the more convinced I am that many, many of us have misunderstood God's instructions in the cultural mandate and that mistake, while not even necessarily our fault, carries some very real risks. Not only is it important that we all understand the truth, but it's also important that we understand the dangers of this misunderstanding, so we can protect and care for the women around us.

Here's the deal: When we think the cultural mandate teaches that the highest calling of women is motherhood, when we believe that it is the heart of our purpose, we create a system in which some women qualify as women of God and others do not. We base a woman's value on something entirely beyond her control. And we essentially establish a club that admits only a few and leaves the rest behind.

Think about that with me. Do girls and young women have value now, or is their youth a waiting period until they can reach their full potential as child-bearers? This misunderstanding leaves behind every young girl, or, worse, it teaches them that they have one, and pretty much only one, thing to offer . . . a womb. It's a burden young women should not have to bear, and yet in many places in the church today, it's a burden that is heaped upon them. When motherhood is the ultimate goal, everything else is just busywork.

What about women who are not married or women who deeply long for children but whose bodies or circumstances just will not allow that? Our friends or sisters or selves who grieve every month? This misunderstanding tells them that they don't measure up, don't qualify, and aren't quite as godly as their child-bearing counterparts. Oh, there are other options, sure. They can pick up the slack by being missionaries or serving in children's ministry (the church always needs more childcare workers) . . . but the underlying message is that they are not quite enough, and that is entirely wrong.

The belief that women are primarily called to have babies creates a hierarchy in which some women simply matter more. As a natural consequence of this interpretation, women who have children are seen as more special than those who don't, and moms are given more attention and more recognition. Please don't get me wrong, I love mom's ministries. We *need* them. But if we're not careful, we can signal to other women that they matter less—less to God, less to us, and less to the church.

But that cannot be. God's plan is not intended to limit, as we'll see. It is intended to expand. It doesn't restrain—it brings freedom! God's plan brings value and worth and hope to all our hearts. He created us with a purpose—to bear his image—and he has given us a plan to carry that out.

Whoever you are, whatever your age or marital status, and whatever the condition of your womb, God has already declared that you are an image bearer. It's woven into the very fiber of your being, and your ability to have children does not influence that fact at all. You are not a better image if you're a mother, nor are you less of an image if you're not.

The heart of our purpose is not to be child-bearers; it is to be image bearers. And God has a perfect plan for how you are to live that out. Which, of course, brings us back to the cultural mandate. If God is not saying that we're supposed to have babies, what is he actually saying?

WHAT IS TRUE

Every passage has a context. And, as the saying goes, context is king. Context helps us to interpret Scripture correctly and to protect ourselves, and others, from heart-wounding misunderstandings. The context of the cultural mandate is the whole creation account, not just the moments surrounding the creation of the man and the woman, so let's put it back there and see what happens.

Genesis 1:1 declares that God created everything and that *he* is the focus of everything to come. Genesis 1:2, as we talked about in chapter 1, provides the framework and presents the themes necessary for understanding what he was about to do: "The earth was without form and void, and darkness was over the face of the deep. And the Spirit of God was hovering over the face of the waters." God will deal with the emptiness by filling, and he will deal with the chaos by bringing order, and he will do it all personally. Starting in Genesis 1:3, we see this happen. As the final act of this process, as the grand conclusion to creation, God declares that he is going to create personal image bearers. Images of himself who will display his character and attributes to the world. Images who will imitate him. After God declares what he is going to do, in 1:27 he actually does it as he creates the man and the woman and creates them in his image.

Throughout the entire process of creation, God fills the

emptiness and brings order, and he does it lovingly and person-ally. And it's in *this* context that he turns to his image bearers and says, "Be fruitful and multiply and fill the earth and subdue it, and have dominion" (Gen. 1:28). Do you see what just happened?!? After spending days filling the earth with all good things, after ordering and caring for all things, the God of creation turns to his new image bearers and whispers, "Now it's your turn!"

G. K. Beale put it so well when he said, "Just as God, after his initial work of creation subdued the chaos, ruled over it, and further created and filled the earth with all kinds of animate life, so Adam and Eve, in their garden abode, were to reflect God's activities in Genesis 1 by fulfilling the commission to 'subdue' and 'rule over all the earth' and to 'be fruitful and multiply.'"[5] These are the words of a king inviting his beloved children to join him, to follow his lead, to do what he did. He calls us to do what images are created to do: imitate!

When God gives the cultural mandate, he's not speaking in a vacuum. He speaks in the beautiful context of *his* work in creation.[6] Do you see that? He is the main character, the focus of all of everything, and he fills the earth and then turns to his images and invites us to do what he did. It's all about him! Yet so often when we read Genesis 1:28, we forget everything that happened to get us to that point. We think of it as a separate call, as if the period at the end of verse 26 concludes that part of the story. Instead, God's invitation, his blessing in verse 28, is directly connected with both his action in creation and his proclamation that humans will bear his image. He is both our pattern and our reference point; he sets the pattern for us to follow in creation, and he enables us to follow it by making us in his image.

---

5. G. K. Beale, *A New Testament Biblical Theology: The Unfolding of the Old Testament in the New* (Grand Rapids: Baker Academic, 2011), 32.
6. Beale, 37.

When we put the cultural mandate back into its context, when we see that his command to fill the earth is all about our imitating God as his image bearers, when we realize that he's calling us to fill just as he filled, we start to understand just how big this invitation is!

FILLING LIKE HIM

It's so easy to read Genesis 1:28 and assume that the call to be fruitful and multiply is only talking about babies. But if this verse is a call to imitate God, we must ask ourselves how God himself filled the earth. What is God calling us to imitate?

When we watch the days of creation unfold, we see God filling the world in a multitude of ways. He fills the seas and the mountains, the jungles and the forests with every creature imaginable. He fills the land with trees and plants and the skies with clouds and stars. The variety of his creation is almost unfathomable! But he doesn't just fill the earth with *things*, he also fills it with music, song, laughter, and dance. He filled the garden with the chatter of squirrels, the roar of lions, the song of birds, the brightest of colors, and the richest of smells. Our God delights in beauty and art; he created stories and poetry and imaginations and flavors.

God created his children, his images, and placed them on the earth; this was absolutely part of the way in which he filled the earth. But we have to see that he did more. He filled the earth in so many ways and then invited his people to do the same. This is what he calls us to imitate! We glorify him by displaying his creativity and by bringing life to the world around us.

The call to fill the earth is about more than babies.[7] Having children may be a part of it, to be sure, but it's not the whole thing.

7. John D. Currid, *Genesis*, vol. 1, *Genesis 1:1–25:18*, Evangelical Press Study Commentary (Darlington, UK: Evangelical Press, 2003), 88.

Rather, the cultural mandate is a stunning, huge invitation to use the unique gifts and talents that God has given each of us to imitate his creative nature and bring his presence to the world. God looks at the image bearers he has created, and he invites them *all* to join him. He's the Lego creator handing us instructions, saying, "Here's how I did it. Now see what you can come up with!"

Filling the World

Art, music, hospitality, gardening, cooking, writing, storytelling, mathematics, programming . . . creating of any kind imitates God! You fill the earth by doing anything that adds beauty and life and fullness to the world around you, whether you prepare a simple meal, start a business, or create a work of art. The job of an image bearer is to use your gifts to mimic the passionate, creative work of God.

Abraham Kuyper, the Dutch Reformer, taught that filling the earth referred to "the filling of the Garden with the products and processes of cultural activity. . . . In that sense, not only the family, but also art, science, technology, politics (as the collective patterns of decision making), recreation, and the like were all programmed into the original creation order to display different patterns of cultural flourishing."[8] Filling the earth is a big, beautiful, huge invitation to imitate God and bring flourishing to the world. Whatever you do to fill the earth and bring flourishing to the world reflects the image of God.

When I think about this type of image bearing, my mom always comes to mind. She's crafty, imaginative, and an incredible artist. When I was little, she encouraged my siblings and me to do any type of art that appealed to us—coloring, theater, painting,

8. Richard J. Mouw, foreword to *Common Grace: God's Gifts for a Fallen World*, vol. 1, by Abraham Kuyper, trans. Nelson D. Kloosterman and Ed M. van der Maas, ed. Jordan J. Ballor and Stephen J. Grabill (Bellingham, WA: Lexham Press, 2015), xxvii.

handmade Christmas ornaments, songs belted out in the kitchen, and puffy-paint sweatshirts. She taught me to see the beauty in everything, even my mistakes. And she showed me that the quality of the product was not nearly as important as the process and the motivations behind it.

For years, she was the event coordinator at a large church in our area. Whenever there was a conference or banquet coming up, she would spend hours upon hours creating beautiful themed centerpieces, welcome gifts, or tablescapes. As a young woman, I once watched her work and felt genuinely confused. It wasn't necessary. We didn't need centerpieces. What did it matter if the goody bags matched the theme or not? When I finally asked her about it, her answer was simple: "We don't *need* pretty things on the table, but I am convinced that people relax more when they feel welcomed and they can listen better when they are relaxed. If I can do something to make people feel cared for and help them to listen better when they come into our church, I will." To her it was about way more than just appearances. It wasn't about the things she was creating; it was about the people who would be cared for in the process. She was using her gifts to image God. She was taking the things that she loved to do and using them for his glory and for the flourishing of others!

God is calling us to do the same. To look at the things we love and the gifts we have and to see how we can use them to bring life to the world around us.

Filling Within

But filling the earth is not just about DIY projects and crafty endeavors; it isn't just about art. It's about bringing abundance to the earth, to your home, to the lives around you. It's about bringing life and fullness to the world. Which means it's not just external—it's internal too. Through mentoring, we pour into another person and build them up. Through discipleship, we draw image bearers closer to God and multiply God's people. Through teaching, we fill minds and hearts with knowledge and truth. The Great Commission in Matthew 28:19–20 isn't a new command; it's a furthering and an expounding of the spiritual aspects of filling the earth. The cultural mandate is rightly seen as the first Great Commission.[9] Anything we do that brings life to the hearts and minds around us images God!

When I was in high school youth group, I was a student leader of one of our small groups, and I led with a woman who became my mentor and is now a very dear friend. We talked every week that year, preparing for the study and praying for the other students. She modeled for me what it looked like to lead well. But even more than that, she poured herself into me. She called me, prayed for me, took me out to coffee. She taught me about the Lord and loved me well through some turbulent teenage years.

On one particular Wednesday night, I arrived at small group more than a little surly. My mom and I had argued before I left that night, and I was upset, so I stood in the middle of my group of friends and ranted about my mother and all the ways she was working to ruin my life (or at least my day).

During my tirade, the calm voice of my mentor broke in. "Elizabeth," she said, "your mom was right, and you were wrong." She went on to gently remind me that my mom was merely asking me to do what I had agreed to do and that by ranting as I was, I was gossiping and disrespecting her. I needed to stop. If those words had been said by almost anyone else in the world that night, I don't think I would have listened, but this was a woman who loved me and had continually pointed me to the Lord. I trusted her and the truth of what she said. I don't know if she knows it, or even if she remembers that moment, but her willingness to live as an image bearer, to fill as God filled, impacted

9. Beale, *New Testament Biblical Theology*, 57.

my life. That night she showed me what it looks like to graciously speak the truth. She was my teacher who taught me about the Lord, about respecting my parents, about repenting, and about grace. She went on to lead the women's ministry at that church, and while *crafty* is not a word I'd use to describe her, she continually lives out the image of God by investing in the lives of women and teaching them to follow him.

Filling the earth is such a huge, amazing calling. Anything you do that builds up, encourages, strengthens . . . it all imitates God's creative work in multiplying and filling the earth.

A MEANINGFUL *MULTIPLY*

When God calls us to be fruitful, multiply, and fill the earth, he is issuing a stunning call for us to imitate him. We fill as he filled! But it's not a onetime sort of thing. The idea of being fruitful implies the ongoing nature of this calling. And the fact that we are called to fill "the earth" implies the far-reaching application of this.[10] It is a calling that applies to all areas of our lives: our work, our homes, the way we impact the culture around us, all our relationships, our mental health, our faith . . . the list goes on and on. It's not just about how we behave in church—it's about the way our lives reflect him.

Imitating God in this way impacts everything. It means continually looking around for ways in which you can use the gifts and talents that you have been given to impact the world. And because we are imitators of God, it means that he is to be our constant guide; we look to him, draw near to him, follow him as our model. Which brings us back, once again, to Genesis 1:2. God filled the emptiness, brought order to the chaos, and did it all in a way that was loving, caring, and personal. The overflowing,

10. Currid, *Genesis*, 88.

outward-focused love—a love that prompted him to create humans in the first place—informs the way we imitate him. To say that we are called to fill like he did is to say that we are called to love the world around us as he does and to be as outward focused as he is.

Filling the earth is not about how creative or talented you feel. It's not dependent on the contents of your craft cupboard (or if you even have one!), or the quality of your covered dishes, or even if you've ever led a single Bible study ever. It's not even about huge, noticeable things. Filling the earth is about bringing life, and beauty, and hope, and truth to the world. It's about little acts of ordinary obedience that use the gifts you have for the flourishing of others. It's about looking to God and imitating him. God has equipped you with specific passions, and he is inviting you to use them for the filling and furthering of the world.

SCRIPTURE TO CONSIDER

Genesis 1:1–28
Psalm 71
Colossians 1:15–20

FOR REFLECTION

1. What has been your experience regarding the command in Genesis 1:28 to be fruitful and multiply? How did you feel when you saw that it was the focus of this chapter?
2. The belief that the call to be fruitful and multiply is one referring to physical babies is extremely common. How have you seen this played out in your life? How has it made you feel? In your experiences, does it feel like there is a hierarchy among women in the church? How does this bigger view of filling confront that?

3. Read Genesis 1:1–26 and write a list of ways you see God filling the earth.

4. Take a moment to think about the things you love to do and things you think you're good at. Do you enjoy singing? Reading? Cooking? Teaching? Being with friends? Whatever it is, write it down. Now, look to see how any of these things reflect the character of God. How is he already using the gifts and passions he's given you to reflect himself to the world? How is he inviting you to use your gifts more?

5. In the questions for reflection for chapter 2, you looked at Colossians 1:15, which says that Jesus was the firstborn of all creation. It also says that he is the "image of the invisible God." As the image of God, Jesus fulfilled the cultural mandate perfectly even though he was never a father himself. Think about his life. How did he fill the earth, and what does that mean for us?

4

THE CALL TO RESTORE

"... and subdue [the earth], and have dominion ..." (Gen. 1:28)

"You want me to what?!?"

My theater teacher looked at me with a hint of a smile. She knew exactly what she was asking and just how hard it was going to be for me.

It was my senior year of high school, and I was a tried-and-true drama nerd. I did the plays and the musicals, I did the dancing and singing, but most of all, I did the backstage stuff. In fact, I loved the makeup, costumes, and stage dressings so much that I had signed up for the tech theater class. I thought it would be a fun way to prepare for all the upcoming shows; it turned out to be so much more.

The assignment that had caused me so much shock was simple enough on the surface. I was to colead a team from our class in cleaning and organizing the prop room. Easy. I loved that sort of thing. There were two problems, however. First, the team was almost exclusively made up of freshmen boys who, as far as I could tell, only took the class for an easy pass. And second, I was not allowed to get off the couch ... the grubby, ancient couch that sat outside with its back to the prop room.

My shock must have shown on my face, because my teacher went on.

"If I let you in that room, you will do it all. The shelves will be labeled and ordered, but you will have learned nothing and neither will the guys in your group."

And she was right. What started as a simple cleanup assignment turned into one of the most meaningful projects of all my years in school, a project I still think about on a regular basis. The thing was, while I saw a disaster of a prop room, my teacher saw *me*. She knew that I was a competent (*arrogant* is probably a better word) student and could have done the project easily, but she also knew that I had completely written off the guys in the team. Where others would have seen a disorganized room, she saw disorganized relationships, and she was willing to do whatever it took to fix that.

That year I spent weeks sitting on that grungy couch, teaching those guys everything they needed to know about organization. In the end, they knew the difference between flora and fauna, knew how to use a label maker, and knew the basics of folding linens. Me? I knew them. I learned their names and found out about their hobbies. I learned how to talk with them, how to encourage them, how to motivate them to finish this massive task. I asked them why they took the class, and I listened to their dreams for the future. I *saw* them.

And seeing them changed me.

Seeing people is hard sometimes. I mean, they're around us all the time, but actually *seeing* them is where it gets tricky. We write them off. We make assumptions. We devise excuses about why they're not worth the effort it takes to get to know them. But image bearers are imitators, and God is not a God of faraway, distant noticing. He's personal. He's knowing. He's a God who loves order—but not just ordered spaces. He's a God who loves ordered lives. He's a God who delights in cultivating hearts. And he's inviting us to join him.

We spent the first few chapters of this book looking at what we are as image bearers. God created us to reflect him to the world. Apart from anything we do or any functions we possess, we simply are his image. But now we've moved on to look at the cultural mandate and the marvelous way in which God invites us to live as his image on the earth. The last chapter explored what it means to be fruitful and multiply. But the cultural mandate doesn't stop there. It goes on. After instructing his people to fill the earth, God says, "Subdue [the earth] and have dominion" (Gen. 1:28).

And once again, things start to get messy.

A SKEWED *SUBDUE*

"And God blessed them. And God said to them, 'Be fruitful and multiply and fill the earth and subdue it, and have dominion over the fish of the sea and over the birds of the heavens and over every living thing that moves on the earth'" (Gen. 1:28). Just like the first half of the cultural mandate, the second half is easily misunderstood. And in the same way that misunderstanding being fruitful and multiplying causes so much suffering, misunderstanding subduing and having dominion does too. So, before we jump to God's actual invitation, we need to understand who was being invited. Who is God addressing in the cultural mandate?

The cultural mandate was given to *both* Adam and Eve and thus applies to all people, both men and women. I mention that because while that may have been obvious to you, it was not obvious to me. Perhaps because the cultural mandate consists of two parts, or because two people were present, or because of God's words to Adam and Eve after the fall—I'm not sure why—I spent much of my life believing that God's command to subdue the earth and have dominion over it was specifically given to Adam. In my head, it was as if God turned to Eve and said, "My daughter, my beloved, your job, your one and only job, is to have babies.

Lots of them." Never mind that there is nothing a woman can do to ensure that happens. Never mind that two people are required. In my head, this verse was saying that a woman's whole job was to have babies. Praise God that I was mistaken, as we've seen.

Then I thought God turned to Adam and essentially said, "Adam, my son, your job is to farm. Work hard, try your best, make sure there is food in bellies and roofs over heads, and you're good." I thought this part didn't apply to Eve at all.

What's more, I thought this was just about work. I thought it was about authority. I thought it was a man's thing.

I was wrong.

When God spoke his plan for us to live as his image, he spoke it to both Adam and Eve, the man and the woman, and it applied to them both equally. Dividing God's plan is not just incorrect; it harms the people around us and deeply impacts the way we view God. This passage is so easily misunderstood, and those misunderstandings cause so many problems. It's important to take a moment to talk about what those problems are, just like we did in the last chapter—not just so we can address them in our own lives but so that we can care for the people around us too.

THE PROBLEMS THAT ARISE

So, what are the problems that come from a skewed understanding of "subdue" in the cultural mandate? Well, first, such a misunderstanding causes division by separating men and women and, in many ways, pitting us against each other. It takes the verse out of the context of creation, it limits God's plan for us, and it creates a dichotomy in which women are praised only for their childbearing and men are praised only for their work. But, as we saw in the last chapter, God doesn't make that distinction.

When we think "subdue" applies only to men and work, we easily judge others for their ability to provide in the ways *we* think they should. We elevate high-paying jobs and act like some vocations are inherently better, or more spiritual, than others. We can easily start to think of the home as a woman's realm and the office as a man's and sometimes, without even realizing it, discourage men from participating in family life at all. The cultural mandate, then, becomes a nine-to-five sort of thing; do it for a while and then hang it up and relax. Do you see the problems this one little misunderstanding can cause? It gets to the very heart of our value and where we get our worth. When we see this verse as just being about work and leadership, we make that our purpose and forget that it's not. Our purpose is not found in our work; it's found in the image of God we bear.

For so long I misunderstood this verse. I thought God was limiting what I could do. I thought it meant that working at home was not important or didn't qualify. Or worse, maybe God wasn't speaking to me at all—maybe because I was a woman, I wasn't needed or wanted in this way. But none of that, as we will see, is true.

The other major problem with this misunderstanding is that it dramatically skews the way we view God. It's so easy for us to confuse the word *dominion* used in Genesis 1:28 with the idea of domination, but when that happens, we start to see God as an angry taskmaster. When we think subduing the earth is just about work, we see him as distant—providing for his people, sure, but then putting his feet up because he'd done enough.

Misunderstanding the cultural mandate has huge implications for the way we see God, but it also impacts the way we see others.

When God gave the cultural mandate, he spoke directly to both Adam and Eve. "And God blessed them. And God *said to them* . . ." This was not a situation of "his" and "hers" commands. God called both of them to live as his image bearers, because they both fully bore his image and they were both created for that purpose. The cultural mandate was the blueprint and the frame around which their whole lives were to be shaped; it was the way in which they were to live out the image of God they bore, the way in which they were to take the glory of God to the whole earth. Separating the cultural mandate along gender lines severely limits what God was saying. God's plan is not to limit, but to increase. His plan for both his sons and daughters is bigger and better and more freeing than most of us realize.

The question then is not just who was given the cultural mandate. The question is, what does it really mean?

THE PATTERN

Most of the time when I hear people talk about the calling to subdue the earth, they talk about taking care of the earth or ruling over nature. At its best, this promotes the idea that we are caretakers of this planet and need to do our best to preserve it. At its worst, this idea has been used to spread the lie that, because we are rulers over it, we can take what we want without regard for the world. Dominion is often tagged onto this discussion as a more specific call to have authority—thus, we take care of the planet by ruling over it. Sometimes it's reduced to the idea of work in general, about how we were created to be active in our vocations or in providing for others.

Most of these are good ideas.[1] Subduing and having dominion does include caring for and protecting the earth. God does this when he blesses the literal ground and brings forth plants from the soil. And having dominion is a declaration of human authority, stewardship, and representation of God on earth. It is all those things. But the context of creation, as we will see, shows us that this command is so much more.

---

1. With the exception of the whole "taking whatever we want" thing. That has absolutely no basis in the Word of God.

Subdue and have dominion . . .

Once again, we have to go back to Genesis 1:2. There we see that God will deal with the emptiness by filling it, deal with the chaos by bringing order, and do it all in an intimate, caring, and personal way. As creation unfolds in Genesis 1:3–27, God brings order on days 1–3 and fills those now-ordered places on days 4–6.

Perhaps it's my love of art, or perhaps it's because we are visual and imaginative beings, but when I read the creation account, it's the filling that takes center stage. I can imagine the stars filling the sky because I've seen the Milky Way in a cloudless night sky. I can picture tropical paradise because I've been to, well, not a rainforest, but conservatories and beaches and places where nature and beauty abound. I can imagine animals wandering peacefully because I've seen a happy dog run to its owner. I have smelled amazing scents, tasted delicious foods, and seen bright colors, so I can imagine all those things combined into one stunning landscape. But order is harder. Despite the fact that order comes before or alongside filling in the creation account, it can be hard to picture. But it's so, so important to see.

The first thing God does is separate things: the light from the darkness, the earth from the sky, and the sea and dry land. As he does so, he names them all. The light he calls day and the darkness night (see v. 5). He calls the expanse heaven (see v. 8). And he calls the dry land earth and the gathered waters sea (see v. 10).

As he starts filling those spaces, he is methodical and organized. He categorizes time by filling the night sky with stars *so that* there would be seasons and calendars and ways of talking about the past and the future. He groups the animals by their kind and plants by theirs. He gave everything a shape, a form, and an identity. He doesn't just create animals, however; he also creates habitats and places for them to dwell. He provides not just food and water but home and safety. In a very real way, God subdues the chaos by organizing and creating places for his creation to dwell. God demonstrates his dominion by lovingly providing for all of their needs, making those places safe and full of peace. He demonstrates that he is a God of order and provision. But what does that look like for us?

Ordered Spaces

Genesis 1:2 says the earth was "without form" and presents a picture of God moving from the macro, big-picture aspects to the fine details of creation. In doing so, he brings order to the wildness, to the chaos, and then he invites us to do the same. On a practical level, this has huge implications for the way we live our day-to-day lives. It means activities such as cleaning our homes, doing the dishes, even folding the laundry are image-bearing activities. They are simple, even menial, tasks, but they bring order to the spaces we live in.

On another level, though, subduing the earth means that the work we do, whatever that might be, matters. Business skills, financial management, customer service, IT, food service, farming, medical professionals, keeping your home, teaching . . . literally anything you do that brings order to the world around you reflects the image of God! Gardening, cleaning up, caring for the environment all matter because they are ways in which we can demonstrate the order-bringing nature of God and ways in which we oversee the care of the world.

So often, though, when I think about organization, I think of keeping things separated and put away; everything has a place, and that's where it needs to stay! Puzzles stay in boxes. Books stay on shelves. Play-Doh is never mixed, and coloring is within the lines. (Not that I can keep my home anywhere near this tidy, but that's what I imagine.) In whatever sphere I'm operating— whether I'm home, in the office, or out and about—it's easy to see the division of an ordered environment. But that's not what we see in creation.

God's dominion is not divisive—it is *unifying*. He gives everything a space to belong to emphasize not division but diversity. In the early days of creation, everything roamed freely. Animals interacted with each other and with Adam and Eve without fear. Eden was not a doctor's sterilized office, white, crisp, clean; it was a wild, busy, loud menagerie of life and joy. It wasn't a place of separation; it was a place of ordered peace. Peace, it would seem, is one of the results of giving everything a place to belong; that is what God created when he brought order to the world. He established spaces for his creation as a way to meet their needs. He cared for creation as a loving Father and benevolent King.

What this means for us is that subduing the earth is about more than ordering environments to keep things clean. It means ordering environments *for the care of others*. It means purposely inviting people in—even people who don't look, or think, or act like us. It means working to make our homes and churches and lives places of welcome and safety. It means joining together to cultivate spaces where people are seen and provided for. This isn't order for organization's sake; it's subduing the chaos so people can flourish.

Ordered Hearts

But God doesn't just care about ordered spaces, he cares about ordered relationships as well. First and foremost in the creation account, he established himself as King and Ruler over all. In fact, the very means by which he created—his word—shows his authority.[2] He is a King who knows, cares for, and provides for his subjects. Then, at the very end of creation, God creates his image bearers and blesses them and calls them to imitate his

2. Courtney Doctor, *From Garden to Glory: A Bible Study on the Bible's Story* (Lawrenceville, GA: Committee on Discipleship Ministries, 2016), 40.

order-bringing care by granting them both dominion as well. By creating us in his image, he established us as vice-regents over his creation.[3]

This is the type of dominion we are called to imitate: life-bringing, caretaking, cultivating peace. Having dominion means more than working hard at your job or taking care of the planet, though these are good things. It means knowing the people around us, seeing them in such a way that we are ready to help to care for them. That's what God does, and we are his image bearers.

The cultural mandate is not a domineering, authoritarian call; it's a command to love well. Imitating God in this way means caring for and seeking to restore relationships. It means protecting those more vulnerable than ourselves in whatever ways we can. It means speaking truth with grace and love and pointing people back to the Lord. When talking about subduing and having dominion over the earth, we need to carefully fix in our minds a picture, not of domination and work, but of protection and cultivation.

God subdued the earth by giving everything a space and a home and a place to flourish. And he had dominion over all things by seeing them, knowing them, meeting their needs, and loving them well. This! This is what he invites us to join him in—not just a vague sense of rule, but a personal care of the people around us. Whatever you do, then, that cultivates peace, loves people, and brings order to the spaces and relationships around you lives out the image of God you bear! When you care for your home, you act as an image bearer, and when you support a hurting neighbor, you display God's image. How beautiful is that!

---

3. G. K. Beale, *A New Testament Biblical Theology: The Unfolding of the Old Testament in the New* (Grand Rapids: Baker Academic, 2011), 37, 82.

SEEN

A few years ago I went through a hard season as a mom. One of my kiddos was struggling, and life was difficult. We met with specialists and teachers, we had plans in place to help, but it was still really, really hard. It was hard feeling "on" every moment of the day, it was hard being a mom to my other children when this took up so much of my attention, it was hard worrying that other people would see little bits of our story and judge me—or my child—harshly, and it was really, really hard watching my little one hurt. I felt helpless. And I was so very tired.

During that time, though, I started to get to know another mom from my church. It turned out that she and I shared very similar interests, our two daughters were the same age, and, perhaps best of all, she lived within walking distance. We started getting together once a week to drink coffee and let our youngest play while our oldest were in school.

On one of these days, the chaos that had been swirling around my life pretty much exploded. I sat on the floor in my upstairs hallway crying as I texted to say that things were not good and I wouldn't be able to hang out that morning. Her response? *I'll be there in five.*

A few minutes later, she showed up with a coffee and a hug, and she watched my other child so that I could spend the morning loving and caring for my struggling one. She met me in my chaos, she saw me, she knew me, she cared for me . . . she walked into some of the hardest moments of my life and imaged God. Her care mirrored the care of my heavenly Father. Her love pointed me back to the God who loves me and my little one more than I could ever understand. She was a beautiful example of what it looks like to be an order-bringing image bearer.

Taken out of context, the cultural mandate is simply a command to have Christian babies and work hard to take care of our families and the earth. But put back into the context of God's example in creation, the cultural mandate becomes so much more. Working hard is good, and it is part of image bearing. But subduing the earth is also about anything we do to create space, to encourage belonging, and to promote peace. It's about holding back the chaos of sin and brokenness that so easily damages the hearts of the people around us. It's about speaking truth into a dying world. It's about flourishing and cultivating healthy relationships in our homes and communities so that others can flourish as well. And at its heart, it's about filling the earth with the glory of God.

Having dominion, then, is not about authority, although that's a part of it. It's about care, and protection, and provision. It's about seeing the people around you. Knowing them and meeting their needs whenever and wherever possible.

That morning, I sat on the floor in my upstairs hallway and listened to my friend downstairs in my kitchen as she got our kids snacks, played games, and was overly excited about their silly, amazing stories. My hair was dirty. I hadn't washed off my makeup from the day before, and I'm pretty sure I was wearing the same grungy shirt I'd been wearing for days. But I was loved, and my family was being cared for, and I cannot tell you the peace that she brought into my life that day.

A BETTER PLAN

I don't know about you, but sometimes life is simply heavy. Sometimes the chaos of this world feels too weighty to bear. But the truth of the matter is, we were never meant to carry it alone. The cultural mandate was given to Adam and Eve together. They were individuals who were created as the image of God and while they each fully bore God's image (and have the dignity, worth, and value that go along with it), they bore it differently, each displaying various aspects of God in various ways. To live out the image of God in its most vibrant and its fullest, they needed to work together—it was not a command they could fulfill on their own. Image bearing is about joining with others for the flourishing of others!

Do you feel the freedom in that?

Where misunderstanding said this doesn't apply to us, God's Word says that it does. Where we limited it to be just about work, he flings the door open and says that it's about imitating him. It's about seeing people, caring for others, pushing back the darkness, and bringing peace to the world around us.

The cultural mandate is a huge blessing—it's an invitation away from all the confusion and the man-made lists we've created about what we're supposed to do to be the people we were created to be. The Creator God who knows you and loves you and sees you is looking you in the eye, smiling with the love of a proud father, and beckoning you to come along.

The confusion and misunderstandings surrounding this verse lead to frustration, loneliness, comparison, and even shame. They can minimize the work we do throughout our lives or convince us that our work, as women, doesn't matter as much. But subduing the earth as God did is not just for men, and it's not just about vocation. It's not about cleaning up the mess; it's about creating places for things to flourish. It's about cultivating the world. It's a call to see others as he sees them and to love them well. Whenever you clean your house or put away laundry, whenever you sit down to listen or reach out to help, whenever you point others back to the Lord, you are living out the image of God. Subduing the earth is about so much more than working hard. Rest in that, dear friend. You are loved. You are equipped. And you are being invited to live as the image you were created to be.

SCRIPTURE TO CONSIDER

Genesis 1:1–28
Psalm 111
Hebrews 1:3

FOR REFLECTION

1. How have you experienced the command to subdue and have dominion over the earth? How has this affected your view of God? Your view of your purpose?
2. Read Genesis 1:1–26 and make a list of all the ways you see God subduing and having dominion.
3. Take a moment to think about your life and the spaces you inhabit (home, work, community, and so on). Where and how do you see chaos or disorder creeping in? Now think about the ways God might be calling you to help to bring order and peace to those places. What would it look like for you to use your unique gifts and skills to reflect him there? How can you care for the places in your life?
4. Think about the people around you. Where and how do you see chaos creeping into your relationships? Is there tension, hurt feelings, uncertainty, fear, and so on? Now think about ways God might be calling you to help to bring order and peace there. What would it look like for you to push against the darkness and image him in your relationships? How can you care for the people in your life?
5. Read Hebrews 1:3. Here, the writer of Hebrews calls Jesus the image of God, the exact imprint of his nature. Take a moment to think about the life of Christ that we see in the gospels. How did he subdue the earth and have dominion over it? What does his life teach us about how we can reflect God's image in ours?

5

THE CALL TO RESCUE

"It is not good that the man should be alone;
I will make him a helper fit for him." (Gen. 2:18)

There was a slight crispness to the air as I grabbed my bag and slipped out of my dorm room. The campus was golden with the early morning sun. The birds were singing in the trees, and I was going to my very first tap class.

Well, first in college. High school musical theater had given me a smattering of experience, a hand-me-down pair of shoes, and enough confidence to convince me that this would be a fun way to use an elective credit. So I signed up. Me! Five-foot, four-inch, somewhat overweight, hilariously uncoordinated me was going to be dancing . . . with other people . . .

Ten minutes later, as the white marble performing arts building came into view, my confidence was evaporating. Who in the world was I to think that I could take tap? I was too out of shape, too odd, too awkward. I would end up on my bum in front of a room full of dancers!

Somehow, and I'm still not entirely sure how, I opened the glass doors and walked into the building. I was sick to my stomach with nerves, shaking, and ready to bolt, but I managed to find the classroom. And that was when something amazing happened. There, warming up before class in front of the mirrored wall was the woman who had choreographed all my high school plays; she was the teacher! I didn't know her well, but she recognized me and immediately invited me to stand near her at the front. I had no idea what a gift that would be.

You see, it turns out that dance—like many things, I suppose—is all about imitation. You watch your teacher, step by step and move by move, then try to do what they showed you. It won't look the same, but that's OK because you're learning. So you try again to mimic their movements. Then you try again, and again, and again. Eventually, what you do will match them, and it will be time to start learning new and more complicated steps. One day, after who knows how long, you'll have learned enough to take all those moves and combine them into your *own* dance. Even though the combinations are different now, the steps still echo back to the one who taught you. Even the best dancers imitate their teachers, and there is a beauty in that type of imitation.

My teacher's invitation for me to stand by her that day was an invitation for me to become a better dancer. She was putting me in a position to see her more and imitate her better. Good teachers do that.

God is a really good teacher. The best, actually. But he's not a God you can follow from far off. Not at all. He's a God who invites us in, pulls us close, and places us near so that we can see his face and, like dance students standing at a bar, imitate him. Because that's what image bearing is all about.

We have been looking at what it means to be made in the image of God; we have seen that we are imitators who were created to reflect the nature and character of God to the world. And we've looked at how the cultural mandate is the blueprint for how we are to live out that purpose. It is God's beautiful invitation to join him in his filling and cultivating work on the earth. But the creation account in Genesis goes on, and there is one more aspect of image bearing, one more invitation, that we need to look at as well.

"It is not good that the man should be alone; I will make him a helper fit for him" (Gen. 2:18). It's a specific call for us as women. It's a stunning invitation to imitate God. But it has also caused more than a little confusion.

A CONFUSING COMPANION

Genesis opens with a zoomed-out, big-picture look at creation—God creates everything. After giving us instruction on how to read the rest of the account, the story zooms in, allowing us to see the events of creation unfold in greater detail. Toward the end, God creates the man and the woman and gives them the cultural mandate. The story of creation then ends with God resting on the seventh day.

Starting in Genesis 2:4, Moses takes us another step closer to the action. This is not a *continuation* of the creation story but another zoom in. Having overviewed all that God created and the highlights of each day, we move in closer to see the details of the sixth day more clearly. You may be very familiar with the account in Genesis 2, but even so, it's worth it to take a moment to go over what transpired.

Here we see Eden, we hear about the rivers and the trees, we see God's personal action even more clearly, and, in that, we see his deep love for his creation and specifically for his image bearers. A little way into the chapter (in 2:7), God creates man by forming him from dust. Rather than simply call him to life, God breathes life into him! He perfectly sculpts the man, Adam, and his very breath causes Adam's heart to beat and his eyelids to flutter. This is beautiful and intimate, unique and powerful. What it is not, however, is a total change from what we saw in Genesis 1. God had declared that he was going to make both men and women, and here we see the detailed process of how he accomplished that.

After forming Adam, God creates the garden, places Adam in it, tells him to work it and keep it in verse 15, and then, in verse 18, says it's "not good" for this newly created human to be alone. God brings all the animals before Adam to name them, and Adam, in an act of reflective dominion, *sees* each and every one and, in naming them, cares for them. But while doing that, Adam realizes there is no creature like himself. He is alone. God then causes Adam to fall into a deep sleep, and from Adam's rib he creates the woman.

All of that may be a review for you. But details of stories, especially when we hear them over and over again, can get jumbled. They did for me. And when that happens, problems start to arise. Big problems. For most of my life, I was confused about three small details that make a huge, huge difference.

The Focus

The first thing I misunderstood is the focus of the passage. For so long, I thought the focus of this part of the story was Adam's loneliness and his need. His desire became the cornerstone of the entire encounter with God. It was not good for him to be alone. He needed Eve. I started to forget what I had read in Genesis 1 and to think that God was moved by Adam's need and responded to it by creating Eve. She, then, became the object of Adam's desire and, first and foremost, the solution to a problem. When seen like this, Eve, while important, is only important insofar as she could fill the void Adam experienced.

The Order

Second, I got the order of events in this passage mixed up. Instead of how it's presented, I thought the story went like this: (1) Adam was created, (2) he named the creatures, (3) he realized he was alone, (4) God realized he was alone, and (5) God created Eve. But this is not how things happened. God decided to make Eve way before Adam realized he was alone. In fact, God declared it was not good for Adam to be alone before Adam even realized he was! God brought the animals before him for Adam's benefit, to prove in a visible and tangible way that he was alone and that his aloneness was not good.

I'm not really sure if this timeline misunderstanding caused the shift in focus or if believing the focus was on Adam's need caused this timeline to solidify in my mind. Either way, both of these are pretty huge misunderstandings with painful results.

The Implications

My misunderstandings shifted God out of the leading role and made Adam the main character of the story, and they shifted God's creation of the woman to little more than an afterthought, a means to an end. It's a subtle thing, one we might not even recognize until we stop to think about it, but it is a shift with massive implications for how we understand what God is doing and what he intends for Eve and for us.

Before we go one step further, allow me to state, for the record, that Eve was not plan B. She was not an afterthought, and she was not merely created to satiate a desire of Adam's. She was made with a purpose, and she was given a way to live that out. As we saw in previous chapters, her primary purpose was not to be a wife or mother (though she would be both, and both are amazing things). Rather, her primary purpose, declared before she or Adam had even been created, was to bear the image of God.

It's so easy to turn to Genesis 2 and forget all we just read in Genesis 1! But Eve was a part of the plan from the beginning. God declared he was going to place his image on the earth and that it would be both male and female. Both men and women would be his image bearers! Up until God brought the animals to Adam, it seems Adam didn't quite get that he was alone. He didn't feel lonely and didn't realize he had a need. God had to demonstrate that to him.

The fact of the matter is, God placed Adam in the garden to protect and care for it, gave him instructions, and, immediately after giving him those instructions, said that it was not good for him to be alone. God moved first. The implication in this corrected order is that Adam didn't need a pretty face or even a friend to fill some emotional void. It wasn't his *loneliness* or his need for a companion that necessitated the woman, it was his *calling*. He wasn't just alone in the garden; he was alone in his mission.[1] He needed a co-laborer, someone to stand with him in carrying out the call to fill and to cultivate the earth as an image bearer. Not only is God's image magnified when we join with others, it was designed to be lived out that way. As image bearers we are to join with others for the flourishing of others.

This misunderstanding had implications for the way I understand the passage, but it also had huge implications for how I understood myself. When I thought that Eve was an afterthought, I thought I was too. When I thought she was only created to be an object of Adam's desires, I objectified myself as well. Confusion, shame, hurt, and comparison have all been big parts of my story, and all find their roots in these misunderstandings. I believed, and I suspect I'm not the only one, that I was inherently less important to the world and to the church than the men around me. But that is not at all true!

The order in which these events take place is one of those details that, when even slightly shifted, greatly impacts our entire understanding. Eve was not an afterthought, and she was not created simply to meet Adam's need. As an image bearer, she had her own unique skills and gifts to use to imitate God in her life and

1. Carolyn Custis James, *Half the Church: Recapturing God's Global Vision for Women* (Grand Rapids: Zondervan, 2011), 109.

display his image. She had a vital role to play in bringing the presence of God to the earth. Her purpose was saturated with dignity and calling, and so is ours.

God placed Adam, his image bearer, in the garden and instructed him to work and keep it. Then, in light of this calling, he declared that it wasn't good for Adam to be alone. Adam needed a co-laborer. He needed someone to join him in his task. He needed a helper. And here again, things start to get messy.

HOPE FOR THE HELPER

I'm not super big on chores or allowances at our house. It's not that I'm against either, it's just that I've never been type A enough to stick to any of my well-planned, Pinterest-worthy charts. We live with the understanding that everyone is both responsible for their own belongings and expected to help out as needed along the way.

The exception to this policy is what I think of as "helper chores." These are extra things my kids can do to earn money if they want to save up for some new toy or Lego set. These are things I normally do, or should do, but will gladly let someone else handle for a whopping total of 25 cents per chore. They are easy, simple, quick chores that give my kids something to do to help without my worrying if they are not done quite as thoroughly as I would have done them myself.

The beauty of these helper chores is that my kids get to learn how to help and how to save financially. The bonus for me is I occasionally get extra help doing things that probably wouldn't get done otherwise. I like my helper chores, and I love my little helpers. But here's the deal: I cringe at the idea of being a little helper myself.

There was a time when the word *helper* meant more than it means today. It used to refer to someone who provided the aid necessary to complete a task or even someone who contributed the strength or means needed to do so. In fact, depending on where you look, that definition is still found in dictionaries today. But the meaning of words tends to shift over time. Particular places and contexts and eras add layers of connotations, and eventually it's possible for the meaning of a word to be slightly, or even vastly, different from what it used to be.

Helper is one of those words. While the above definition is still used, more and more people don't recognize it. Now, the word has become associated with the type of work children do—sweet, endearing, but unnecessary. When we hear it, we think of "Mommy's little helper," a small child who desperately wants to be included but really just needs to be kept busy. Instead of emphasizing the type of help brought and the strength contributed, the meaning has shifted to focus, almost patronizingly, on the lack of real help given. In fact, *Merriam-Webster* even defines it as "one that helps; especially: a relatively *unskilled* worker who assists a skilled worker usually by manual labor."[2] Unskilled. Ouch.

Quite frankly, I don't want to be a helper like this. I don't want to be kept busy and out of the way so that other people can do the "real" work. I want to matter, to make a difference, and I want what I do to matter. Something in me longs to believe that I have made an impact and the world is a better place for my having been here. I think we all feel that way because we are image bearers who were created as the image of God; reflecting him and bringing flourishing to the world around us is what we were created to do!

Yet for so many years, when I read "I will make him a helper fit for him," I was confused. I knew God wasn't making Eve less valuable than Adam; I'd heard enough talks to know that. But I

2. *Merriam-Webster*, s.v. "helper," accessed November 16, 2018, https://www.merriam-webster.com/dictionary/helper. Emphasis mine.

also didn't know what it meant, and I didn't know how "helper" could possibly be something for me. I mean, if that's what God planned, sure, I'd try to get on board, but it still didn't seem to fit.

I'm not ashamed to say that I have tuned out a large chunk of women's talks that dealt with this verse because it simply hurt. I wanted to believe God had good plans for me, that he loved me, chose me, and called me. I wanted to believe that I was "his workmanship, created in Christ Jesus for good works, which God prepared beforehand, that [I] should walk in them" (Eph. 2:10). Basically, I wanted to believe the rest of Scripture, but I couldn't figure out how the love presented everywhere else fit with this almost belittling word presented right at the beginning of everything.

But there is so much more going on in this verse than part-time summer help or dusting-the-baseboards-so-Mom-can-actually-get-stuff-done help. As is so often the case, God's plan for us is bigger and more freeing than that. To understand his love and his plan, we need to understand what is really being said when God declared that he would make Adam a "helper."

CALLED AN *EZER*

You are more than a little helper. You were created to be an ezer!

What is an ezer? *Ezer* is the Hebrew word often translated as "helper"[3] in Genesis 2:18, and it's a little word with a lot of meaning. In fact, it's really hard to translate because we don't have a single word in modern English that captures all it entails. While "helper" is not a bad translation, it's not quite complete either, and we really, really need to understand the fullness of what it's trying to say.

---

3. Sometimes you'll see it translated "helpmate" or even "helpmeet."

As a verb, the word *ezer* can mean to help or bring aid.[4] But it can also mean "to save from danger" or "deliver from death."[5] It carries with it the idea of protecting and giving encouragement. It's often grouped with other words that imply a sense of urgency and a rushing to bring necessary assistance to those who need it; it conveys the idea of running with great speed and without hesitation. As a noun, it refers to the one who brings that aid.

What's more, *ezer* comes from two Hebrew root words, one which means "to rescue" and the other which means "to be strong."[6] Based on that, some scholars have argued that a better translation than "helper" is actually "power," as in, Eve was to be a power stronger than the animals who could bring aid to, and join with, Adam.[7]

On the surface, that seems very clear. Ezers are helpers. But, as I hope you can see, they are not little helpers. They bring dramatic, necessary, life-saving aid. Their protection means the difference between achieving victory and being completely, totally overrun. It is no small thing to be an ezer. But there is more to it than even that.

Ezer, as a noun, is used twenty-one times in the Bible—twice in Genesis to describe Eve, three times to talk about nations sent by God to rescue Israel, and sixteen times to refer to God *himself*. But what's more, almost every time it is used to describe God, it does so in a military context;[8] he is rescuing his people

---

4. James Strong, *The New Strong's Exhaustive Concordance of the Bible* (Nashville: Thomas Nelson, 1995), "ezer."

5. Victor P. Hamilton, *The Book of Genesis: Chapters 1–17* (Grand Rapids: Eerdmans, 1990), 176.

6. R. David Freedman, "Woman, a Power Equal to Man," *Biblical Archaeology Review* 9, no. 1 (January/February 1983): 56.

7. Freedman, 57.

8. Carolyn Custis James, *When Life and Beliefs Collide: How Knowing God Makes a Difference* (Grand Rapids: Zondervan, 2001), 186.

from their enemies (see Deut. 33:7). He is saving them from destruction. God is Israel's help (see Ps. 70:5) and shield (see Ps. 33:20); he delivers them from the sword (see Deut. 33:29). He is their defender, their strength (see Ps. 20:2); he even rides through the clouds to rush to their side (see Deut. 33:26)! God does not sit on the sidelines, waiting for instructions or direction or an invitation to join in. God is not an assistant who hopes his contribution matters. He is their God. Our God. He is the rescuer of his people, and this is how he chooses to describe women as well.

What's more, God didn't just say he was going to make Adam a helper, he declared that she would be a helper "fit for him." The word there is *kenegdo*, and it's used only here and in Genesis 2:20. While it is often translated as "fit for" or "according to" or even "appropriate to," a more literal translation is "as in front of him (or according to what is in front of him)."[9] Outside the Bible, in later Rabbinic Hebrew, it is simply translated as "equal."[10] The implication here is that Eve was not created simply to work for Adam or be beneath him in any way. Rather, she was his equal, his counterpart. Equal in status as an image bearer. Equal in blessing in the cultural mandate. In every way able to join with him in their calling to rule over the earth as God's regents.

It can be so easy to read Genesis 2 and think God is putting a box around Eve and women. We act, maybe without even realizing it, like this idea of being a helper is a restriction meant to give her something to do or keep her in her place. But that is the complete opposite of what is going on. Rather than limiting Eve, God beckons her to greater freedom. Rather than restricting what Eve is allowed to do, God throws the door wide open and says, "Come, be like me!"

9. Hamilton, *Book of Genesis*, 175.
10. Freedman, "Woman," 57.

When God declared that he was going to make the woman and make her an ezer, he firmly, and for all time, rooted his plan for her in himself. We are to be ezers like he is an ezer. In the context of Adam's living out the image of God he bore, fulfilling the cultural mandate by filling and having dominion over the earth, God declared that he needed an ezer. A life-saving partner. A true co-laborer. Someone who was his equal in power, value, and calling. Someone who would join with him.

The calling of an ezer is an image-bearing, mandate-fulfilling calling eternally based in God himself. It is a picture of the strength, the mindset, and the disposition we are to have toward the people around us and the work that is to be done. It is a cry to protect and defend those who need it. It is a reminder that we are desperately needed and an invitation to join with others and join the fray. It is no small thing to be an ezer.

MODERN-DAY EZER

The question, then, is, what does that mean for us today? I don't know about you, but I don't own a sword. I sort of wish I did because that'd be cool, but I don't, and I can't pick up a literal shield to defend the people around me either. So how are we able to imitate God in this way? What does it look like?

Well, if being an ezer is a call to imitate the life-saving, aid-bringing character of God, then being an ezer means first and foremost, jumping in. Image bearing means we will join with others, but this goes deeper: it implies rushing to protect. It means looking for the vulnerable in our midst and helping them. It means watching to see where God is working and being willing, eager even, to join him. It looks like partnering with your brothers and sisters in Christ to serve others. It's jumping in when there is a need you can meet and rushing to take care of others when they are hurting.

When I think of ezers, I think of the women I know who bravely stand against injustice— whether in a courtroom, a town-hall session, or a voting booth. I think of moms who attend IEP (Individualized Education Program) meetings to advocate for their children. Daughters who fight for their aging parents. And friends who sit with weary neighbors. I think of the woman who reports her abuser and those holding her hand while she does. Of volunteers at crisis pregnancy centers, food banks, and shelters. Of women standing up for the truth. I think of anyone who willingly rushes to care for others.

I think of the woman at my church who grocery shops every week to send food home with kids who live in areas of high food insecurity. And another who joined the Parent-Teacher Association to be a voice for kids whose parents couldn't. It's my friend who started an organization to rescue women out of sex trafficking. It's my friend who faithfully delivers meals when families in our community are struggling. Being an ezer doesn't mean we all run to the other side of the world; it means our eyes are open to the needs around us. Being an ezer means knowing that who you are and who you were created to be are important, valuable, and necessary to the work of filling the earth with God's image and bringing flourishing to the world around us.

This isn't a "how to be a good wife" message. This is a divine picture of who we were created to be. That's why the order of events matters so much. God declared Eve an ezer in the context of Adam's being unable to fully carry out the cultural mandate alone; it was not good for him to even try. We each use our unique abilities, but we use them best when we join with others for the flourishing of the world. Ezer applies to all areas of our lives: all our relationships, our ministries, our families, our work, and our homes. And it applies at all times of our lives: from childhood all the way through our adult years.

This is image bearing at its most valiant. We, as women,

are being called to imitate the aid-bringing, support-offering, protection-bringing, life-giving work of our God. God calls us to join with his people, men and women, wherever we are, whatever our context, using whatever unique gifts we've been given to protect those who need it. We rush with great speed to the rescue and care of the body of Christ, and we do that with the strength, dignity, and courage of an image bearer.

For so long I tried to be the woman I thought I was supposed to be. I volunteered at everything, served everywhere, and exhausted myself in the process—because that's what good Christian women do, right? But understanding what it means to be made in the image of God changed that. I started to see that I was loved and valued, that I was given a calling and equipped to carry it out. I understood that as a woman I wasn't plan B or a second-made, second-best citizen of heaven. No, I was loved and valued and important to the work. God values his daughters! Not just because they make it possible for others to do the real work, but because they are desperately needed to complete the work as well. Being an image bearer is the heart of who we were created to be, and being an ezer is part of how God planned for us to live that out.

Being an ezer isn't an adult thing, it isn't a wife thing . . . it's an image-bearing thing. Before women ever walked the earth, God declared he was going to make an ezer and he was going to make her female. She was created to run to the aid of her people, to protect those who needed protection, and to fight to save those who were in danger. She was the perfect co-laborer who could stand with other image bearers, joining with them to reflect God's image to the world.

You were made with a purpose—to be an image bearer of God. You were created with a plan—to fill the earth, to bring order to the chaos, and to model God's rescuing love to a world in need. You, my dear friend, are an ezer.

SCRIPTURE TO CONSIDER

Genesis 2:4–25
Psalm 70
Psalm 121

FOR REFLECTION

1. What has been your experience with Genesis 2:18? Misunderstanding the order of events in the creation of Adam and Eve and the reason God created Eve in the first place can have huge implications for us. Describe ways in which this confusion has impacted you. How has it affected the way you see God? The way you see yourself?

2. How does an understanding of the word *ezer* change the way you understand Eve? How does it impact the way you view yourself? The women around you?

3. It wasn't Adam's loneliness that necessitated Eve; it was his calling. Does this focus on living out the image of God together change the way you see your role? What are some ways in which you join with the people around you to carry out the cultural mandate? What are some ways you think God is calling you to do so?

4. Take a moment to think about the community you are a part of. Who are the vulnerable, the hurting, and the struggling? Where are the image bearers who need someone to come alongside them? What would it look like for you to care for them or bring them aid?

5. Read Psalm 70 and Psalm 121. In what ways do you see God bringing aid to his people? These are just a couple passages in which God is described as an ezer. What do these passages communicate about God as an ezer? What does that mean for us?

PART 2

RESTORED

6

THE PROMISE HE MADE

"I will put enmity between you and the woman, and
between your offspring and her offspring; he shall bruise
your head, and you shall bruise his heel." (Gen. 3:15)

When I was a child, one of my favorite places in the world was the library. In all honesty, it is still one of my favorite places. But back then, when I was small and the shelves were big, when words were new and stories unread, the library was downright magical. All those shelves filled with books that could take you to faraway places and see unimagined things! All those adventures, all those stories! I would walk up and down the aisles and let my mind run wild with the possibilities.

Among those aisles and bookcases, there was a version of Beauty and the Beast that I loved more than any other. I have no idea how many hours I spent poring over it, but I do know it had illustrations unlike anything I had seen before. Each page had a picture of the story as it unfolded: Beauty meeting the Beast, Beauty interacting with the enchanted staff, and so on. But on most pages, hung behind the characters, a tapestry or a piece of art depicted the exact same scene—only as if the enchantment had been broken. If Beauty was talking with the Beast, an image behind her showed Beauty talking with the prince. If the enchanted staff (changed into animals in this version) were serving her, in the background was a picture of them doing the same actions as human beings, free of the spell that had bound them for so long.

As a little girl I would wonder, if a tapestry like that were hanging behind me, right at that moment, what would it show? What would people see if they could see the real me? If everything was the way it was supposed to be? You see, I wanted to be like Beauty, but even as a child I could relate so much more to the staff. Bound. Hidden. Fully aware that the "me" people could see was not the real me, not the me I wanted to be.

I still feel this way sometimes. I want to be the plucky heroine who sacrifices everything and shines brightly for the world to see, who lives in freedom and flourishing. But more often than not I feel a little bit bruised, a little bit sad, and oh so weary. Have you ever felt that way?

I think of this especially when I think of image bearing because everything in me knows, just as I did as a child, that all is not how it should be. I know that I was created to be the radiant image of God—to display his character and nature to the world and to live as his reflection. But I also know that something went horribly, devastatingly wrong. Where there was supposed to be peace, there is conflict and strife. Where there was hope, there is now shame; where there was intimacy, there is now comparison; and where there should have been freedom, burden resides instead.

We've been diving into the words of Genesis to see the splendor of God's creation, his majesty, and his amazing plan for us. And it really is amazing. But every time I read those chapters and study those events, I also feel a little sad because we're not in Eden anymore. Maybe you've felt the same thing. We know that there is a problem, that something went wrong. But, as we will see, God is not going to leave things this way. Because while there is a problem, there is an even greater promise: a promise of restoration.

THE INTRUDER

The pages of Genesis open with creation. By nothing but the power of his word and his will, God calls all things into being. As the stunning apex of his work, he declares that he will make humans, both male and female, for a specific purpose. They will bear his image.

We've seen that by the very nature of our creation, we reflect the character and nature of God, and we are deeply loved and valued beyond what we could ever realize.

The opening pages of Genesis fill me with so much joy, and yet, at the same time, something in my heart knows that all is not how it should be. I know that when I check the news and hear reports of crime and hate, or when I talk to a neighbor and learn of sickness and death. I know that nothing is the way it was in the garden. The stunning beauty and the immeasurable peace that existed in Eden is gone.

God placed the first man and woman, his unique image bearers, in the garden. Everything was "very good"—perfect, in fact. Adam and Eve walked with God, felt the gladness of his smiles, heard the subtle reverberations of his voice. They knew his love. But some time later, and we don't really know how long, another figure appears in the garden. An intruder.

We know from elsewhere in Scripture that the snake that spoke to the woman that day was none other than Satan, "a murderer from the beginning" and "the father of lies" (John 8:44). He is called "the ruler of this world" (John 12:31), "the evil one" (Matt. 13:19), "the prince of demons" (Matt. 12:24), and "the god of this world" (2 Cor. 4:4). He was once an angel in the courts of God, but he did not want to be under God's authority.

He longed to be god of himself. Satan led a rebellion, forever declaring himself an enemy of God, and was cast out of heaven.

In his anger at the Lord, Satan comes to the garden with a specific purpose: to deceive and attack those who bear God's image. To separate the Creator from his creation. To murder the ones God loved and blessed above all others. It's still his goal today.

His plan is simple—take them down. The people God created with a purpose; the ones he loved with an eternal love; the ones he chose above all other creatures, above even Satan himself, to bear his image . . . take them down. Satan could have attacked with any number of weapons, but all he needed were a few well-placed words. A single idea, really. A question.

"Did God actually say . . . ?" (Gen. 3:1).

That word *actually* always gets me. It's so sneaky. It's the kind of word you throw in to look innocent when in reality you are anything but. It's loaded with doubt-causing questions. Actually. "Do you actually know what God said, Eve? And did he actually say that?" It seems so simple on the surface, but his words reek of accusation. They cause Eve to doubt both her knowledge of God's command and the goodness of God in giving it. "Why is God holding you back, Eve? If he really loved you, wouldn't he want you to have all good things? Who does he think he is to tell you what you can and can't do?"

Before Satan even uttered a lie, he whispered a question that planted a doubt. A doubt that still echoes in all of our hearts today: Does God love me? It's the doubt from which so many of our struggles arise. The exhaustion we feel trying to measure up, the shame we feel when we believe we haven't, the loneliness when we're convinced we're the only ones. It is a doubt that subtly affects everything, even our very purposes as images of God. Like the master deceiver he is, Satan ensnared God's children and set the stage for his attack.

THE LIE

What follows is a conversation. A horrible, depressing, never-should-have-happened conversation. Eve enters into the conversation and seems to defend[1] God and the boundaries that he gave her and the man, boundaries that God (as their King and Father) had every right to establish. But Satan is a master liar, and he catches her in her own words.

> But the serpent said to the woman, "You will not surely die. For God knows that when you eat of it your eyes will be opened, and you will be like God, knowing good and evil." (Gen. 3:4–5)

What was planted as a doubt is now harvested with a lie. God had told his children that if they ate the fruit of the Tree of Knowledge of Good and Evil, they would surely die (see Gen. 2:17). But now, face-to-face with God's image bearers, Satan accuses God of being the liar instead. What's more, he paints himself as their friend, their ally. Where God was holding them back, he's going to help them to soar. It's heartbreaking.

1. Many people would point out here that Eve misquotes God. They say either she heard God's word correctly but did not take it seriously, or she was told incorrectly by Adam (as she was not present when the instructions were given). I find it more likely that she was paraphrasing in the same way that Jesus and his apostles do in the New Testament (see Luke 4:18–19 vs. Isa. 61:1–2, for example); if that is the case, she did nothing wrong. Carolyn James presents another option, arguing that Eve was actually fulfilling her role as ezer in her initial interactions with the serpent, the problem coming only when she made herself the reference point rather than God (Carolyn Custis James, *When Life and Beliefs Collide: How Knowing God Makes a Difference* [Grand Rapids: Zondervan, 2001], 194–95). Whatever the case, the writers of Scripture comment only on the fact that she was deceived and through that deception, she sinned (see 1 Tim. 2:14). The writers of the Bible do not ever condemn her handling of the Word of God. It is wise for us to follow their lead and refrain from condemning her as well.

Satan's goal, as we already talked about, is to separate God's children from their holy Father, so he twists God's words and plants the lie. You will not die, he tells them, and the reason is simple: God is holding out on you. He could make you more than you are, but he doesn't want to share.

With one statement, Satan questions God's authority: who is God to tell you what you can and cannot eat? He questions God's love: if he really loved you, wouldn't he give you all good things? But he also suggests that the man and woman are missing something, that the image they bear is incomplete. They are *kind of* like God, sure, but not *really* like him. God didn't love them enough to make them all the way like him; he was holding them back. With a few choice words, Satan convinces God's precious children that the image they bear is lacking, that God doesn't love them enough to fix it, but that on their own they could. We have been trying to fix ourselves ever since.

Eve listens to the lie, sees the fruit, questions her God, and makes her choice. Adam, who stands at her side, does the same. She doesn't persuade him, doesn't coerce or seduce him—she merely holds out a piece of fruit, and he takes it. He heard Satan's word, he stayed silent, he made his choice. And nothing would ever be the same.

THE CHOICE

When Adam and Eve ate the forbidden fruit that day, sin entered the world and the hearts of mankind. Innocence was gone. Relationships, destroyed. Death had come, and the beauty of the garden was dimmed. All hurt and shame and sadness and exhaustion can be traced to that one moment. In that instant, everything went wrong.

Sin does that. It's messy and painful, and it leaves waves of disruption in its wake. And because it's such a huge deal, and because it all started at the fall, it's worth pausing to talk about what sin is, what it did to us, and where we were left as a result. Because we know, like little children reading fairy tales, that there is a problem. It's a problem that affects not just our relationships with God, but our purpose in this life as well.

So what exactly is sin? I grew up believing that sin is either doing what God told you not to or not doing what he told you to do. Simple. Easy. And that is a pretty good explanation. But unfortunately, that's where my understanding stopped: sin is an action or inaction and nothing more. The Bible, however, paints a much darker picture of sin, one that we must understand in order to understand the problem, to really get what went wrong with the world and understand how our purpose was distorted. Sin, according to the Bible, is not simply what you do, it is why you do it. It's a heart thing. In other words, sin is not just a practice, it's a posture.

Was the fall a moment of disobedience? God told Adam and Eve not to do something, and they did it anyway? Yes, but it was also more than that. Adam and Eve made a choice. When they chose to eat the fruit, more than choosing mangoes over apples, they chose self over God. They rejected God's authority, his rule over their lives, and his plan for them and chose instead to be the ones to decide what was right and wrong, to have knowledge of good and evil for themselves.

They weren't duped into eating a pomegranate; they made a strategic decision to be in charge. To be gods. Sin is not so much doing or not doing something—it is a heart condition that puts anything and everything above God. It's a rejection of his authority over our lives. What happened in the garden that day was outright rebellion. It wasn't that they didn't know God's Word; it was that they chose not to believe it. Sin is ultimately a suppression of the truth and a rejection of God (see Rom. 1:18).

But what then does it do to us? When Adam chose to rebel, the Bible says that sin entered the world and entered all our hearts (see Rom. 3:23). All people everywhere throughout all time and history have sin in their hearts. What's more, apart from Christ, every single thing we do is marred by sin (see Rom. 3:10–12). That means that even the nicest, most kind, most "good" thing someone does, without Christ, comes from a heart that is fully bent on rejecting God's authority. Sin corrupts everything.

Sin is not passive either. It lords over us (see Rom. 6:14), enslaves us (see Rom. 6:6), reigns over us in death (see Rom. 5:21). We can do nothing to escape its hold over us, and the reality is that while sin reigns in our hearts we do not want to. Sin is both an action and a condition, and it totally and completely separates us from God. Forever. Without any hope of finding our way back and without any desire to, even if we could. Sin, to be clear, is not just about what you do, it's about your heart.

Sin completely and utterly separates us from God. But it also introduces a whole host of other problems. All the hurt, pain, suffering, disease, and death start here. All the shame, comparison, loneliness, hurt, and confusion radiate from this moment. We may be familiar with what sin did to our relationship with God, but we must also understand what it did to our purpose, what it did to our ability to live out his image.

THE RESULT

When I was a little girl, my dad gave me a snow globe with a delicate ivory angel standing inside. When you shook it, tiny snowflakes and iridescent glitter swirled before floating down to settle at her feet again. To me, it was magical. I quickly gave it a place of great importance on my "special things" shelf in my room, where it lived until the day I moved out of my parents' house.

Years later, I carried moving boxes up the steps into our

family's new townhouse in the heat of a September morning. You should know that September in the DC area is not really fall, more like summer's angry sister who comes into town uninvited, and it was staggeringly hot. My children toddled around the empty rooms while I went back and forth between the moving crate and the front door, dripping with sweat and brimming with frustration. Nothing had been going my way. I walked up the flight of stairs to get to the main floor and had just made it to the porch when the bottom of the box I was carrying gave out and the entirety of its contents fell to the ground.

Old journals, a trophy or two, and some childhood pictures scattered to the side undamaged. But lying in a puddle on the concrete was the angel. I think my heart may have been right there with it. The glass dome had completely shattered, and the angel had come off her base. I kneeled down, picked her up, and did nothing to stop my tears.

It was still my snow globe, but it was broken. It wasn't unrecognizable; I knew exactly what it was and what had gone wrong. But it wasn't able to do what it had been created to do—not well, at least.

When sin entered the world and the hearts of God's image bearers, it crashed against our purpose like the pavement against my snow globe. It didn't remove or even destroy the image that we bear, since being made an image of God is intrinsic to who we are as humans and is not based on our ability to live it out. (In fact, God reaffirms that just a few chapters later in Genesis 9:6.) But, because sin affects our ability to ever choose God, it disastrously affected our ability to live as image bearers in the way we were created.[2]

---

2. George C. Hammond, *It Has Not Yet Appeared What We Shall Be: A Reconsideration of the Imago Dei in Light of Those with Severe Cognitive Disabilities* (Phillipsburg, NJ: P&R Publishing, 2017), 180.

Image bearing is all about God. But how can we reflect God when the mirror is broken? And if image bearing is about him and sin means we will always choose not-him, or will outright reject him, you can see the problem. When Adam sinned, sin entered our hearts, and our ability to live out our purpose was disastrously marred.

Thankfully, being made in God's image is not about what you do, it's about who you are.[3] You were created as God's image. That means that from the moment you were given life, you were his image bearer, totally and completely apart from anything you can do or can bring to the table. And that brings so much hope! It means that sin and the consequences of sin, whether mine or others', even the natural fallenness of the world, cannot stop us from being the image of God. That's also why we can say that all people, everywhere, no matter what, are God's image bearers and thus have infinite value, dignity, and worth.

We are all made in God's image, but sin makes it impossible to fully live that out. While bound to sin, we are separated from God. We were created to shine with the radiance of his glory, but that image is now flawed, tarnished, and broken. Like my snow globe, it's not gone or utterly unrecognizable, but neither can it do what it was created to do.

Adam and Eve ate the fruit. They listened to the lie and chose to believe a creature rather than their Creator, a talking snake over their loving Father. And when they did, the Bible says that their eyes were opened, because, you see, not everything Satan said was a lie. Eating the fruit really did give them the knowledge of good and evil. They knew. They knew the depth of what they had done and the goodness of the one they had done it to. So they hid. And for those terrible, horrible moments, it looked like evil had won.

But God . . .

3. Hammond, 185.

THE SAVIOR

Adam and Eve did the one thing God told them not to do. When they ate the fruit, they rejected his authority. When we read the account in Genesis, we should wonder if anything can be done. Will God step in and fix what has gone wrong? Because this is his story! God is the main character, the protagonist, the hero. If anyone is going to fix this problem, it must be him.

When God comes to find Adam and Eve that day, it's an edge-of-our-seats moment. What will he do? He would be well within his rights to walk away. But God! He calls Adam out of hiding, he gives his children a chance to confess, and then, in a dramatic turn of events, he turns his wrath not on his image bearers who had just rejected him but on his enemy instead.

When God comes to the garden that day, he doesn't come as a disappointed dad or an angry king. Like the protagonist of all good stories, the God of the universe enters as the ultimate hero, the only one who can make things right again. By coming as he does, the Creator of heaven and earth is saying, "I will fix this." But what's more, with the words that follow, the Holy Father looks down on his enemy, his arms out between his children and his foe, and says with a hushed fury, "You cannot have them. They. Are. Mine."

Stop for a moment and let that seep in. Adam and Eve had made their choice. Sin had entered the world and with it shame and fear and loneliness. It drove God's children into hiding; it damaged the very image they were created to bear and their ability to live out their purpose. Yet God doesn't turn to them first. There's no frustrated sighs or guilt-inducing accusations. He doesn't turn his anger on his children; he turns to his enemy instead.

The God of the universe unleashes his wrath on Satan and issues a curse. *Curse* is an extremely strong word. I forget that sometimes because we talk about "curse words," by which we mean words that our grandmas wouldn't approve of or angry words without any real power. But *curse*, as it is used in the Bible, is an expressed desire that extreme misfortune fall on someone. It carries the idea of deep loathing. When God curses, his curse also carries an eternal promise, for what God wills always comes to be. So when God looks at Satan and says, "Cursed are you," he isn't making idle threats. His curse is a promised action that is as good as done. For all intents and purposes, it has already happened.

I love what Courtney Doctor says about it: "In essence, what God is saying is, *even though you, Satan, have just defeated my children, I am going to send One who will not just defeat you, but will completely destroy you. The war is on and I will win.*"[4] God turned his wrath on Satan because his heart was already for his children.

God looks at Satan and lays on him the curse to end all curses: he will be totally, completely defeated. The curse is a promise—a promise we desperately need. "I will put enmity between you and the woman, and between your offspring and her offspring; he shall bruise your head, and you shall bruise his heel" (Gen. 3:15).

There are three parts to the curse against Satan: (1) God will put enmity (or hostility) between Eve and Satan, (2) God will put enmity between Eve's descendants (God's people) and Satan's, and (3) a specific descendant will strike the killing blow, thus finally and completely defeating Satan. It's a stunning declaration and one of the most beautiful and grace-filled passages of the whole Bible, and at its heart is the idea of rescue and restoration.

God will move through time and space and history to rescue his people from the chains of sin and redeem them to himself. Where sin left them utterly alone, completely separated from him, where they could not move an inch toward him, he will come,

---

4. Courtney Doctor, *From Garden to Glory: A Bible Study on the Bible's Story* (Lawrenceville, GA: Committee on Discipleship Ministries, 2016), 65. Emphasis original.

wrap them in his arms, and bring them home. And where sin had shattered the image they bore, where it made living out their purpose impossible, he will make all things new and restore all that was lost,[5] including the image they were created to bear and their ability to live out their purpose. And he will do it through the person of Jesus Christ.

THE IMAGE OF GOD

When Adam and Eve stood before God that day, they stood completely mired in their sin. Like peasants staring up at a castle wall they cannot hope to climb over, like servants bound by a curse they can never undo, they were utterly stuck. Their relationship with God was ruined. Their purpose as image bearers was forfeit. But when God issued the curse to Satan, he set in motion a plan to make all things new again. He promised that his one and only Son would come into the world and stand in his people's place so that he could bring them home again. And we see that promise fulfilled in the New Testament. Christ came, fully God and fully man, to live the sinless life we couldn't live and pay the price we couldn't pay. Christ, the very fullness of the image of God, the second Adam, made it possible for us to be with God again. Through his life, death, and resurrection, we can be restored as children of God. We call that *redemption*—we have been redeemed, or bought back. Christ restores the relationship with God that was destroyed in the garden.

What's more, through him, the image of God is being repaired in his children as well. We call this process *sanctification*; it's the way in which the image of God in us and our ability to live it out is being restored. It is "the work of God's free grace,

5. Jerram Barrs, *Through His Eyes: God's Perspective on Women in the Bible* (Wheaton, IL: Crossway, 2009), 46.

whereby we are renewed in the whole man after the image of God, and are enabled more and more to die unto sin, and live unto righteousness."[6] Sanctification means that we can honor, love, and obey God. What's more, it means we will want to. We won't do it perfectly, of course, we will still sin and stumble. But it means we are being made more and more like Christ. We can live out our purpose as image bearers again! Where sin once made it impossible to follow him, where once we could not hope to carry out the cultural mandate, now, through him, we can. His image in us is being repaired. We are being made more and more like him.

But while our salvation is a onetime thing, this process of being made more and more like Christ is not. It really is a process. That means it's not easy. It means confusion and hurts and sin still play a part in our lives. We get discouraged and find ourselves reverting to old ways of living.

In the next chapters, we're going to look at how Adam and Eve responded to God's presence and his declaration. And we'll look at how the ways they struggled in those moments mirror the ways we struggle too. But just as we opened the first section of this book clinging to the truth of God's love, we need to open this second half by clinging to the truth of his promise. He will restore. He is moving in his children to make them more and more like him. There is so much hope!

Where fear once reigned, he is bringing his love. Where confusion dominated, he is bringing clarity. Where chaos filled our hearts, he is bringing order, and where we were empty and alone, he is filling us with his love. He is still the God of creation, the God who brings order and who fills, and he is inviting us to join him again.

6. The Westminster Shorter Catechism, answer 35.

SCRIPTURE TO CONSIDER

Genesis 3:1–15
Romans 3:21–26
Ephesians 1:3–14

FOR REFLECTION

1. Make a list of words that come to mind when you think of the fall. What evidence of the fall do you see in your everyday life? How does that make you feel?
2. Describe a time in your life when you doubted God's love. You're not alone in that—we've all been there! What happened when you felt that way? What happened to change that feeling? How does seeing God's response to Adam and Eve impact the way you can relate to him in your own doubts and fear?
3. Based on what you read in this chapter, write out a definition of sin. What does the rejection of God's authority look like in your life? How have you seen it impact the lives of others? How have you experienced God's grace?
4. God promised in Genesis 3:15 that he would send a rescuer. It was a promise to defeat sin and death and make a way to bring his people home and, in doing so, restore in them the image they bore. How does that make you feel? How does this promise affect your life today?
5. Read Ephesians 1:3–14. Write a list of all the things Paul says Christ has done for us, and then take some time to thank God for the ways he is working in you to make you more like him.

7

THE SNARE
OF COMPARISON

The man called his wife's name Eve, because she
was the mother of all living. (Gen. 3:20)

Once, many years ago, my husband and I were invited to Sunday dinner (fancy lunch?) at the home of a well-known pastor. Now, I say "well-known," but the truth was he wasn't well-known to me. I knew next to nothing about his denomination, didn't know anything about him, and had no idea that in some places of the world "First" in front of a church's name is a big deal. I just knew that a family that loved the Lord was opening up their home and including us.

We accepted the invitation happily, but as we got closer to the day, things started to get a little difficult. While I might not have sensed the importance of this invitation, some of the people around me did. Friends' suggestions and comments about what I should wear and how I should act left me questioning myself and my ability to fit in. Their ideas about what I should say or do or bring left me wondering if I was good enough, or smart enough, or even spiritual enough to go.

By the time the day rolled around, I was a mess, and what was supposed to be a pleasant afternoon with a gracious family turned into one of the most awkward events of my life. I have no idea what I said or even if I said anything at all. I do remember looking down and thinking that my shoes were from the thrift store and wondering if anyone in the stunning, perfectly decorated home would look down on me for it. I was nervous, self-conscious, and shy. I couldn't relax, felt foolish for not knowing what to do, and questioned everything I did. And the thing is, they did have family traditions I wasn't aware of. But when they patiently and kindly explained them, rather than seeing my hosts welcoming me into their world, I grew frustrated and hurt. Rather than feeling included, I felt embarrassed and small.

What could have been a beautiful memory is now one of painful comparison. I was so focused on comparing myself to this family, to seeing if I measured up, that I missed the blessings of that afternoon. I looked at their lovely home, their beautiful clothes, their special traditions, and I decided I wasn't pretty enough, I wasn't godly enough, I wasn't a good enough woman to be there. I compared myself and decided that I didn't fit in. And then, just to make the afternoon even worse, I decided it was their fault. You see, after comparing myself and finding myself lacking, I began comparing the family to my own standards of how *real* godly people should act. I tried to justify my feelings of hurt, anger, and frustration by deciding that they weren't gracious enough, they weren't understanding enough, and they absolutely weren't loving enough.

The problem that day wasn't that the family did things differently than I expected. It wasn't that my friends did anything wrong by asking about my plans, and it wasn't that I couldn't afford nicer things. The problem was not out there at all. It was an inside thing, a heart thing. It was a problem of comparison—a problem that goes all the way back to the garden.

WHERE IT ALL WENT WRONG

When God finished creating everything, he declared it very good. But as we saw in the last chapter, something went wrong. An intruder came, and he planted a lie. God's children chose to believe the serpent rather than their holy Father. They ate the fruit, sin entered the world, they were separated from God, and their purpose was shattered.

It was the darkest day in human history. But it was also one of the greatest days, for, as we saw, it was the day God promised to restore his children. We looked at that promise and what it means and how Christ brings us back to God and restores the image we bear. God's promise runs through every moment of Scripture, and it is a promise that we must hold on to as we move forward. For while we know God has saved us and is restoring his image in us, we also know that we don't always live like that. We sin, and we struggle. But understanding God's love and his purpose for us frees us to draw closer to him and live as the images he created us to be.

The stunning thing is, though, we aren't alone. Right after sin entered the world, Adam and Eve made choices that we, without even realizing, imitate all the time. Looking at how God responded to them teaches us much about how he is working in our own lives today and how he is freeing us, once again, to be imitators of himself instead.

We left off in Genesis 3:15 as God curses Satan. But to see what I'm talking about here, we need to take a very small step back to verse 7. Adam and Eve both ate the fruit, their eyes were opened in understanding, and "they sewed fig leaves together and made themselves loincloths." Sin was now present. Relationships were being shattered, and comparison was rearing its ugly head.

The Image of God

We've said it before: we are image bearers of God. He is the basis for our whole existence, and he is the original in which everything we are and everything we are called to do is rooted. And he, by his very nature, is relational. As his image bearers, we were created to reflect that part of his character, which means we were created to dwell in unity within families, friendships, and communities. Being relational isn't just something that we ought to do or something that can bring us happiness; it's woven into the very fibers of our being. Being made in the image of God means that we were made for closeness. We were designed to need others and to be needed in return. He is the standard for what we were created to be; he exists in perfect relationship and intends for relationships to characterize us as well.[1]

We were created as unique individuals, each full image bearers, but something divinely beautiful happens when we join with others—the image of God is displayed in a new, glorious way. This is what Paul is talking about when he describes the church as the body of Christ—we are all uniquely gifted but working together, in relationship, to display the image of God to the world (see 1 Cor. 12:12–27).

All of this means that relationships are important both to our hearts and to the image we bear. Perhaps that's why Satan hates our relationships so much—because they display the very nature of God. Even from his first moments in the garden, he sought to drive God's people apart—to separate us not just from God but from each other as well.

It's not surprising, then, that one of the first effects of sin we see in the fall is the deterioration of relationships.[2] And while we

1. John F. Kilner, *Dignity and Destiny: Humanity in the Image of God* (Grand Rapids: Eerdmans, 2015), 217.

2. George C. Hammond, *It Has Not Yet Appeared What We Shall Be: A Reconsideration of the Imago Dei in Light of Those with Severe Cognitive Disabilities*

know our relationship with God was utterly severed, the first relationship in the text that we actually see damaged is the relationship between Adam and Eve themselves.

Damaged Relationships

In the early verses of Genesis, we see Adam and Eve dwelling together naked and unashamed. Their relationship was marked by vulnerability—but not the uncomfortable vulnerability that is the stuff of nightmares. It was a vulnerability that was marked by total, complete, and loving acceptance. They saw each other and loved each other without hesitation. They had nothing to hide and weren't afraid of criticism or condemnation. It was love, pure and simple!

But when sin entered their hearts, all that changed. Not only do we know of the effects of sin from the rest of Scripture, but we see it painfully illustrated when "the eyes of both were opened, and they knew that they were naked. And they sewed fig leaves together and made themselves loincloths" (Gen. 3:7). Where once they were naked and safe in that vulnerability, now they scurried to cover themselves. The knowledge they'd gained didn't just reveal the heights of the glory of God and the depth of their crime against him, it also revealed their capacity to betray, hurt, and wound the people they loved. If they could so easily turn from God, what was to stop them from betraying each other? What was to stop someone else from doing it to them? Suddenly, their vulnerability was terrifying. They were exposed, able to be hurt by one another at any moment. And so, to protect themselves from each other and to hide their vulnerability, they crafted loincloths and hid.

When presented with the fruit, Eve saw that it was good for food, that it was delightful to look at, and that it was very desirable

---

(Phillipsburg, NJ: P&R Publishing, 2017), 180.

(see Gen. 3:6). She considered the fruit before her and compared it to what she wanted, what she expected, and what she deemed good. Was it good enough for her? Was it better than the other options? This is what comparison is all about. To compare two things is to evaluate them to determine which, based on whatever standards you are using, is better. Eve compared the fruit of the tree to other fruit she could eat. She compared Satan to God. And she compared the offers they were both making with what she believed she deserved.

Comparison is not a bad thing, in and of itself. We do it all the time—every time we make a decision, actually. However, we must make sure that we're comparing the right things. The comparisons Eve made were not based on the truth of who God is. Instead, she based her decision on a lie, a lie that said God didn't love her enough. Rather than make God the standard for truth, she set herself (her longings, desires, opinions, and so on) up as the reference instead. Evaluating decisions is necessary and good, but we must root our decisions in the truth. And yet, so often, that's not what we do. We make ourselves the reference point, and everything crumbles.

Damaged Purpose

Adam and Eve were united in their vulnerability, but they were also united by their common purpose. God placed them in the garden with the command to carry out the cultural mandate. In fact, as we saw in chapter 5, when God created Eve in Genesis 2, he did so not in response to Adam's loneliness but in response to his calling; it was not good for Adam to try to carry out the cultural mandate on his own. He needed a co-laborer to image God alongside him.

Together Adam and Eve were to display the radiance of God's image. Together they were to create, to restore, and in doing so to bring flourishing to the earth. Together they were to exist in relationship, in community. But sin shattered that. Sin destroyed their ability to live out the cultural mandate, and therefore the co-laboring that was intended to bring them joy now brought them strife. Dominion would now be marked by domination. Where there was to be love and joy and peace, there would now be fear and hurt and anger. And we feel the effects of that today.

Sin separates us from each other. It shattered the relationships we were created to be in. We were designed for a loving community, but sin left us alone and vulnerable (in a bad way). It created hostility where once there was peace. It pulled us into spirals of fear and anger and resentment. There is judgment and blame where sin reigns; deception and backbiting prevail.

But God! Just as we saw God call Adam and Eve out of their shame, he also calls them back into community. He is the restorer of all things, even relationships.

Sin opened the door for comparison, to be sure, but not all comparison is directly caused by sin. In fact, much of the comparison we experience is rooted in misunderstandings instead.

THE PROBLEM OF COMPARISON

I opened this book by telling you about a time when I was overwhelmed by the weight of trying to be the Christian woman I thought I was supposed to be. I sat on my bed and wept because I believed that I would never measure up, that I could never be as godly or as spiritual as the women I saw around me. That moment of exhausted desperation grew out of years of misunderstanding what my purpose was. And at the heart of it all, I had missed the idea of being made in the image of God. I didn't understand God's plan for me, and, as a result, I lived in a state of near constant comparison. The more I talk with women, the more convinced I am that I am not the only one to deal with this.

When we don't understand who God created us to be, we

fall back on ideas that we have created ourselves. Instead of reveling in the beauty and uniqueness in which we were created, we watch other people around us, take in messages from books and talks, even observe the women in the Bible, and come up with a picture of what a truly godly woman looks like. We come up with lists and ideas about what women should do or how they ought to act or what committees they need to serve on. We evaluate the women near us to decide if we like what they're doing or not and then apply that evaluation to ourselves. We rank and compare ourselves to others in a vain attempt to decide where we stand in the hierarchy of women in the church. Are we as good as that woman over there? Are our kids better behaved? Do we serve more or less? How godly are our prayer requests? Is our marriage more holy? We compare the people around us to both the standards we've come up with and the lies we've believed, and when we do this, someone always gets hurt. Sometimes we hurt others because comparison causes us to judge them harshly. Other times we get hurt because we find ourselves lacking.

Comparison, it turns out, is a thief that robs us of joy and pushes us away from community. It lingers in our hearts, evaluating and ranking and dividing the people around us. We wield it like a sword and wear it like armor, attacking other women in our midst and protecting ourselves from their attacks.

Without necessarily meaning to, or even noticing what we're doing, we come to a place where the only way to gauge our value, our identity, and our worth is to compare ourselves to others. Problem is, comparison destroys community—the two simply cannot exist together. You cannot have places of safety and peace and unity and love when you are wrapped up in evaluating and judging and ranking. We were created to live in relationship with others, and we were created to both live in peace with the world around us and to work to establish peace as well. None of that can happen, though, when we're trying to measure up to the women around us. Thankfully, a deeper understanding of what it means to be made in the image of God and what it looks like to live out our purpose frees us from the trap of comparison and invites us to live in community. Praise God for that.

RESTORED

Comparison causes a jagged separation that wounds our hearts and prevents the type of intimate relationships and life-giving community that we were created for and that we need. But, praise God, he didn't leave us there.

Adam and Eve were sinking in their sin. Their relationships with God and each other were shattered, fear reigned over them, and so they hid. But God came. He moved through the garden that day, and, as we saw in the last chapter, he called them out and turned his wrath on Satan. He issued a curse against his enemy and a promise for his people: he would restore them.

The verses that follow are often called "the curse," but the glorious truth is God's words aren't a curse at all. God specifically curses Satan and the ground, but he does not in any way curse Adam and Eve.[3] God does not curse his children; he has already blessed them. Instead, he speaks the consequences of their choice, because there *are* consequences. Death has entered the picture; the image he created is damaged; his plan for Adam and Eve to live out their calling is now filled with hardship, pain, and strife. Sin brought sorrow into the world, and God, as a loving father and perfect king, uses those sorrows to correct and humble and bring his children back to him.

When I thought of these verses as a curse, I assumed there was a hardness or a vindictiveness to God's words. But there is

---

3. John D. Currid, *Genesis*, vol. 1, *Genesis 1:1–25:18*, Evangelical Press Study Commentary (Darlington, UK: Evangelical Press, 2003), 132.

not. God reaffirms the cultural mandate and describes how life in a fallen world will make its outworking more difficult.[4] The man and the woman's desires to subdue and fill the earth would remain, but fulfilling them would now be marked by hurt, frustration, and pain. The outlook is bleak, but God speaks tenderly to Adam and Eve even as he condemns sin and issues consequences. He speaks with tender mercy to his image bearers as he holds back the chaos, overpowering the grief of sin with his gentle love.

Because of sin, living out God's image and bringing flourishing to the earth will not be easy, and there will be times when the very ground is against them—but the call remains. The honor of being made in the image of God remains. The invitation to live out God's purpose on the earth remains. And Adam and Eve felt that! God did not wield consequences like a weapon but beckoned his children into his glory. He restored his relationship with them, restored their relationship with each other, and renewed their calling. And, in doing so, he destroyed the need for comparison at all.

RENAMED

In response to this gracious reaffirmation of their purpose, Adam renames Eve. Whereas up until this point she had simply been called Woman, meaning "from man," he now calls her Eve, which comes from the Hebrew word meaning "living thing." In

---

4. Wendy Alsup and Hannah Anderson, "Toward a Better Reading: Reflections on the Permanent Changes to the Text of Genesis 3:16 in the ESV Part 3," *Theology for Women* (blog), September 30, 2016, https://theologyforwomen .org/2016/09/toward-better-reading-reflections-permanent-changes-text -genesis-316-esv-part-3.html. For more information, see also Wendy Alsup, *Is the Bible Good for Women? Seeking Clarity and Confidence through a Jesus-Centered Understanding of Scripture* (Colorado Springs: Multnomah, 2017), 59–74.

essence, she would be the mother of all life.[5] The life-bringer. She would not be known by where she came from or even for the mistakes she had made: she would be known for God's promise for her future. She would be known for who she is in him. So often when we think about Eve, we remember her sin. But her very name is meant to remind us of God's promise and her restoration!

Can you feel the hope in that? Adam, who only moments before had blamed her for everything that had gone wrong, who thought she was the problem, now chooses to believe instead what God has said about her. What's more, she who is so easily blamed for causing the break in relationships will be the one from whom all community will flow. How beautiful is that?

We, as restored image bearers, are called to be restorers of community as well. God beckons us away from comparison, away from the confusion that exists when we don't know who we were created to be, and calls us to see others the way he does. For when we see others as image bearers, we can love them well, serve them humbly, and join in the type of community we were designed for. It means we can forgive as we have been forgiven and show grace as it has been shown to us.

Although sin once separated us from God, we have now been united to him in Christ, his promised rescuer. And although sin divided us from each other, we can now live in stunning community. But unity doesn't mean uniformity. We are not all the same. We have different gifts and different personalities and different stories, and all of that is important! We are different, but together we are the family of God and together we image him (see 1 Cor. 12:12–27). As individual members, we make up the body of Christ.

This picture of beautiful diversity goes all the way back to the garden, back to those first moments when we saw God, the

5. Currid, *Genesis*, 138.

Creator God, calling into being a world made up of a myriad of differences. Diversity was whispered in his creation of individual, unique image bearers. It was declared in his call for his people to be priests to all nations (see Ex. 19:6). And it was shouted from the rooftops in the epistles as the truth of Jesus is taken to the Gentiles (see Eph. 3:6).

We are different people from different nations, different families, and different backgrounds. We have different hair, skin, and eyes. We wear different styles, like different things, cook different food, and listen to different music. But we are the body of Christ, the children of God, and we were created to be joined together, in him, as a unified people. A community and body of believers.

In Christ, relationships are restored and we can live in community with one another. We should no longer compare ourselves or be competitive with one another (even within our own church ministries!) because we are members of one family, united in Christ and being joined together in him (see Eph. 2:11–22). We are fellow citizens, and we're able to do the good work that he created us to do (see Eph. 2:19, 10), and there is no better job, no more important ministry. Everyone is needed and important. This is the type of loving, caring, accepting, supporting, life-giving community we were created to have and to be.

FROM COMPARISON TO COMMUNITY

A few years ago, I did something I'd wanted to do for a very long time: I made and wore a costume to a comic con. Yes. You read that right, I dressed up as a character from a computer game I loved and wore that costume to a local comic book convention. Yes, I am a total geek. Yes, it was one of the best days of my life. And yes, I am totally proud of the work I did to accomplish that. I spent over a month preparing: studying pictures of the character, drafting a pattern for the clothing pieces, sewing them together, and adding details by hand. I worked hard and was proud of what I had created, and I loved wearing my costume to the convention and connecting with other people just as geeky as myself.

After the convention, I came home and, in my excitement, I posted pictures of my husband and me on my personal social media page for my friends and family to see. What I forgot, however, was that my family had just started attending a church plant in our area, and I had recently friended my new pastor. Fast-forward a few weeks. I was gathering my things after church when that same pastor pulled me aside to introduce me to a couple that was visiting that week. He introduced the newcomers, then turned to them and said with excitement, something along the lines of, "This is Elizabeth; she wears costumes to conventions!"

I'll admit, a huge part of me wanted the ground to swallow me whole. But another, stronger part of me was overwhelmed with gratitude. Rarely have I felt as accepted and welcomed as I did in that moment. It was one of those times when I felt, really felt, that I didn't need to fit the mold. It didn't matter if I looked the same as the other women in our church, or had the same hobbies, or liked the same things. I didn't feel as though I had been compared to them, and I didn't think I was less spiritual or less godly than anyone else. Instead, I felt seen and known, and I felt like part of a community. Knowing that the pastor wasn't comparing me to others in the church helped me not to compare myself either. Instead of feeling uncomfortable, awkward, and shy as I did at that fancy lunch all those years before, I stood in that high-school auditorium turned church sanctuary and felt like a valued member of the body of Christ.

As image bearers of God, we can bring healing and hope to the people around us. Instead of breaking people down, we can build them up. Instead of ranking and evaluating them, we can welcome and serve them. We can love those who seem hard to love. Care for those who are often overlooked. Welcome every person in our midst. We can demonstrate love, offer forgiveness, and create places of peace. We can praise the ways God is moving in the lives of the women around us, be thankful for the ways they are different from us, and joyfully relinquish those things that are not ours to hold on to. And we can rest in the unique way God created us rather than long to be something different, because we are valuable just as we are.

The misunderstandings that surround our purpose push us into places where we compare ourselves and others, and comparison destroys communities. But God through his grace is patiently calling us out of comparison and inviting us to imitate him. The beautiful truth is that relationships thrive when we live out the image of God we were created to bear. Understanding our purpose to be the image of God changes our hearts and can radically change the world around us!

SCRIPTURE TO CONSIDER

Genesis 3:7–20
1 Corinthians 12:12–27
Ephesians 2

FOR REFLECTION

1. Describe a time when you were caught in the snare of comparison. How did it make you feel? How did it affect your relationships with the people around you?
2. We saw in this chapter that one of the first effects of sin in the garden was the deterioration of relationships. What does that look like when it happens? How have you seen relationships deteriorate in your own life? How have you seen them deteriorate in the lives of the people around you? Do you see God working to restore those relationships?

3. When we don't understand our purpose to live as God's image, we easily compare ourselves to others in order to figure out what our purpose should be instead. We come up with lists, sometimes without even realizing it, of what women ought to do, be, or say. What are some things you have heard or believed about what it looks like to be a woman of God that is rooted in comparison rather than image bearing?

4. How does comparison affect relationships? How does a deeper understanding of our purpose as image bearers free us from the snare of comparison?

5. Do you believe that comparison is a struggle in your own life? If your answer is yes, know that God, in his grace, is calling you out of that trap. What would it look like for you to rest in his plan for us as his unique image bearer? What would it look like for you to join God in working to restore the relationships and communities you are a part of?

8

THE SHAME THAT BINDS

And the LORD God made for Adam and for his wife
garments of skins and clothed them. (Gen. 3:21)

The round folding tables had been covered with crisp, white tablecloths. There were burlap table runners and mason jars filled with wildflowers. There were even handwritten welcome cards and beautifully printed out agendas. In effect, the large room normally reserved for the youth group had been totally transformed into a once-monthly retreat for women in our church. A table covered with breakfast food stood in the corner, and flowed in abundance as women mingled, ate, laughed, and enjoyed being out of the house that morning. And I joined them. Sort of.

I laughed with the women at my table. I hugged ladies who had been a part of my life for more years than I could remember. And I chitchatted along with everyone else, repeating my normal answers with a chuckle and a smile: "fine," "tired," "growing like weeds and keeping me busy," and "yes, the traffic on the parkway is going to put me over the edge too!" They were my standard replies, fine-tuned after years of practice. They were safe. They were light-hearted enough to be friendly but honest enough to appear sincere. And they were total hogwash. OK, maybe not totally, but close.

You see, when I had gotten ready for the breakfast that morning, I had painted a smile along with my lipstick and tried my best to stuff everything else away. That was how I did women's events. It wasn't that I didn't *want* to be more real or to be able to talk with someone—after so many years of playing my part, I didn't know how. I was afraid that if I started talking, I would never be able to stop. That if the tears began, I would drown in them. How could I tell these women who seemed to be doing so well that I was doing so poorly? How could I ask for prayer for my kids who were struggling if their kids were excelling at everything? Oh sure, I could share prayer requests that were safe and looked the part, but I couldn't be fully honest. I couldn't tell them that I was struggling: struggling to read my Bible, struggling to worship, struggling to believe that I was anyone God would want.

I wasn't trying to lie to these women; it was just that I was deeply ashamed of my shortcomings, of the ways I was far less or far too much than they were. They, with their designer jeans and manicured nails and well-mannered children, seemed so much better than I was. They were better mothers and better wives and better Christians than I could ever hope to be.

To be very clear, I love women's ministry events. A lot, actually. And I love burlap and hand-lettered inspirational messages. This had nothing to do with what was being said or the environment that was being fostered. It had everything to do with my heart's deep misunderstanding of who I was and who I was created to be. I didn't understand my purpose, and so I compared myself to all these other women in hopes of measuring up, and when I didn't, I was deeply ashamed. Ashamed of my struggles. Ashamed of my shortcomings. And ashamed of all the ways I was failing at the Christian life. Shame, it would seem, often dwells on the heels of comparison.

In the last chapter, we talked about comparison: it is the natural result when we misunderstand our purpose, and it is totally destructive to community. And we looked at the comparison that happened in the garden and how God, by creating us as image bearers and by inviting us to imitate him, calls us out of that trap. Now we're going to move one more step into the story to see another result of the fall: one more area where misunderstandings about the image we bear lead to heart-wounding problems. We're going to look at shame.

THE SHAME

Everything was very good in the garden. God had created a vibrant world of ordered peace, and he'd created a garden especially for his children to dwell. But an intruder came, a lie was believed, and sin entered the world and the hearts of all mankind. Adam and Eve ate the fruit and when they did, "the eyes of both were opened, and they knew that they were naked. And they sewed fig leaves together and made themselves loincloths" (Gen. 3:7).

"Their eyes were opened" is another way of saying they now understood. Exactly what they had hoped would happen had happened. They did have knowledge of good and evil. They did become a little bit more like God. But rather than bringing them the power and autonomy they hoped for, rather than making them more like God in the way that they wanted, this knowledge brought them a deeper understanding of the goodness of God and the evil of sin. They understood, at least in part, the enormity of what they had done, whom they had done it to, and what they were capable of doing still. Once they had had no shame; now they were brimming with it. They hurriedly crafted coverings out of leaves to hide their bodies, and their vulnerability, from each other. Then they took to the bushes to hide from God. Shame had arrived in the garden and in the hearts of mankind.

What Shame Is

The question that must be asked, then, is, what is shame? If we're going to talk about the shame Adam and Eve felt in the garden and the shame we experience today, we need to clarify exactly what we are talking about.

Shame is that "intensely painful feeling or experience of believing that we are flawed and therefore unworthy of love and belonging—something we've experienced, done, or failed to do makes us unworthy of connection."[1] Flawed. Unworthy.

It's important to note that shame is different from embarrassment. Embarrassment is a form of self-consciousness, a feeling of foolishness that is typically surface level and quickly resolved. Embarrassment is like a bruise to your pride. And shame is also different from guilt. Guilt says I *did* something wrong—shame whispers that *I am* wrong.[2] Guilt is knowing that we have behaved in a way that is not in keeping with what we know to be right. Guilt can be a good thing[3] because it pushes us toward reconciliation, but it's not shame.

No, shame is not guilt, and it's not embarrassment. It's deeper and thicker and more damaging. Shame sinks into the most vulnerable parts of ourselves and coats the tiniest crevices of our hearts. It's painful and lasting and changes not just the way we behave but the very way we see ourselves. Shame is intensely intimate and personal; it gets to the heart of who we are and says that who we are is bad. It convinces us that we are not worth pursuing, not worth knowing, not worth loving, and not worth forgiving.

I don't know about you, but I know what it's like to feel

1. Brené Brown, "Shame v. Guilt," *Brené Brown* (blog), January 14, 2013, https://brenebrown.com/articles/2013/01/14/shame-v-guilt/.

2. Brené Brown, "Listening to Shame: Brené Brown," posted March 16, 2012, YouTube video, 20:38, https://youtu.be/psN1DORYYV0.

3. Brown, "Shame v. Guilt."

shame. I know what it's like to sit in the dark and feel utterly, completely, unimaginably unworthy. I know what it's like to listen to the lies that whatever I did or whatever was done to me has left me without worth. I'm not worth helping. Not worth saving. And probably, if I'm honest, not worth loving either. And this, this shame, is exactly what we see happening in the garden that day.

Shame in the Garden

When Adam and Eve ate the fruit and their eyes were opened, they saw the great chasm between who they were created to be and who they had become, saw the gulf between the holiness of God and the darkness of sin, and saw the depths of what they had done. Rather than let that push them closer to God, they dove for the bushes. Genesis 3:8 tells us that rather than run to the Father whom they knew and who loved them well, they hid instead.

With fear entangling itself in their hearts and shame choking them like a twisting vine, they heard the sound of God in the garden. That sound had only ever brought them joy and sent them running to meet him. But not anymore. They had never seen God's wrath, but they knew the depths of his goodness and knew the depths of what they had done. So they scrambled to hide from their Lord.

Shame convinced them that hiding from God was the only thing to do. It told them that he could never respond with love, that they weren't worth loving anymore anyway. Shame whispered that their sin was too big for God and that he couldn't, no, *wouldn't* fix this. Shame told them they didn't deserve to be fixed in the first place. It pushed them away from the one who created them, knew them, saw them, and loved them still. Shame debilitated them. But God is not the God of shame, and shame is not the end of their story.

INVITED OUT

After Adam and Eve made themselves clothes out of leaves, they heard God moving through the garden, so they hid from him. Now God calls out to Adam and asks him where he is. But remember, this is not a normal friend stopping by; this is the omniscient, omnipotent Lord who knows all things. He knows where Adam and Eve are, he knows what has happened, he knows the lie that has been spoken, and he knows the choices that have been made. He even knows what he is going to do to make everything right again. He knows! So when God calls out to them, he isn't asking for his own benefit. He is asking for theirs. This is a chance to come out and to confess,[4] to receive his grace.

We talked in chapter 6 about what happens next. Adam and Eve eventually come out of hiding and start finger-pointing and blame-casting and trying to justify things that never should have happened in the first place. It is not a comfortable conversation! And at the end of it, instead of turning in anger to his children, God turns his wrath upon Satan instead and, in doing so, promises to put an end to sin and death and bring his children home.

In the midst of that curse and that promise, however, is an extremely significant moment for Eve, one that shows us how God responded to the shame that was so tightly wrapped around her.

In verse 15, God says that he is going to put enmity between the serpent and the woman, between Satan and Eve. This is a specific statement with a direct application to the two of them. On the surface, it seems self-explanatory: Eve and Satan will be enemies. Of course they will! We all know that Satan is the enemy; he's the obvious bad guy of this story, so why would they not be?

4. John D. Currid, *Genesis*, vol. 1, *Genesis 1:1–25:18*, Evangelical Press Study Commentary (Darlington, UK: Evangelical Press, 2003), 123.

In fact, for most of my life I skimmed over this part, but this is so much more important than I realized!

You see, Eve has chosen her team. She was on God's side, but given the option of shaking off his authority, she chose "freedom" and switched. For all intents and purposes, when she ate the fruit, she removed herself from God's protection and leadership and allied herself with Satan instead. He was the one who made all the big promises, implied that he would help her, that he had the knowledge she needed, that he was willing to do what God wasn't. He was supposed to be there for her. She chose him.

We don't know exactly what is going on in Eve's mind and heart as she stands before the King waiting to hear what he will say to her, but I wonder if in this moment Satan feels like her only hope. She stands before God deeply ashamed of her actions, so ashamed that she has tried to hide from him! She is aware that she doesn't deserve his forgiveness, aware that she has been deceived, aware that even her husband has blamed her. She is more alone than she has ever been, ever. Who else can she to turn to but the one who started this all in the first place? She knows Satan has lied, but he still wants her, if only just to use her to get to God. But here, in this moment, God says no.

Eve's heavenly Father looks at his beloved child and says, "You will not stand with him. I will not let that happen." God's curse that puts enmity between Satan and Eve is a declaration that Satan is not victorious. He may have won this battle—humanity may be separated from God for a time—but he is *not* going to win the war. And it is a declaration to Eve that all is not lost. Satan will face resistance because God has still chosen Eve.[5] No matter what she has done, God still wants her. He loves her. And no matter how dark things seem, how alone she feels, all is not lost. God is

5. Jerram Barrs, *Through His Eyes: God's Perspective on Women in the Bible* (Wheaton, IL: Crossway, 2009), 45.

going to ensure that even though she can't yet be with him, she won't be with Satan either.

Eve is being suffocated by her shame, but God calls her out. And he doesn't call her out to rub her face in it. He calls her out of the bushes, out of her shame, to offer his grace and remind her of his love. But it doesn't stop there. To me, the most amazing thing about this whole story is what comes next. Not only does God call Adam and Eve out of their shame, he also removes it altogether.

RESTORED

I have a very clear picture in my mind of what happens next: Adam and Eve run from the garden in fear, wearing furry skins in the loincloth style of cavemen. I may have seen it on a Sunday school coloring page or maybe it's from a children's Bible somewhere along the line, but when I get to this verse, this is what I see. Fear. Fur. And running. I see a moment marked by bloodshed, sacrifice, rushed patchwork construction, and a push out the door.

But what actually happens is far more loving, far more intimate, and far better than I imagined. In a dramatic show of grace, God does one more thing for Adam and Eve—he clothes them.

Genesis 3:21 says that God "made for Adam and for his wife garments of skins and clothed them." I don't know about you, but I often get caught up in the word *skins*. I see that and immediately try to figure out where God got them. Was it a sacrifice? Was this atonement for their sin? And while those are good questions, they are not the questions God answers here, and, if I'm honest, I don't think they are the point of the verse anyway.[6]

---

6. I have often heard it said that this is where God set the standard for substitution atonement and blood sacrifice. And while there are a number of

How the garments were made isn't the point. The point of the verse is the *gift*.

The Hebrew word for *garments* used in Genesis 3:21 means "coat, garment, or robe," but it's most often translated as "tunic."[7] Typically it described a piece of clothing that had long sleeves and flowing skirts.[8] It's used twenty-nine times in the Bible: once here with Adam and Eve, eight times for Joseph's multicolored coat, six times to describe the clothing of various other people (Solomon's bride in the Song of Solomon, Potiphar's wife, and so on), and fourteen times to describe the tunics specifically crafted for the priests themselves.

The majority of the time, this word is used for beautiful, important garments. Far from the hodgepodge, patchwork loincloth and slip I pictured Adam and Eve wearing, the clothes God crafted for his children were more likely beautiful tunics. They weren't just a minor upgrade from leaves to fur. They were the equivalent of going from a bike with flat tires to a Tesla, from Garanimals to Gucci.

The word for "skin" is important too. It's the same word used for the covering of the tabernacle[9] and points to our ultimate covering in Christ. So when God gave his image bearers this new clothing, it wasn't a humiliating reminder of their shame and their sin. No, it was so much better than that!

---

reasons why this understanding makes sense and may be what's going on here, the text simply doesn't elaborate on the nature of the actions taken by God to create his gift for Adam and Eve. The term *skin* is used later on in the Old Testament when talking about the ritual sacrifices, but it is also the same word used to describe the coverings of the Temple (Currid, *Genesis*, 139). So while a sacrifice may have taken place, the text emphasizes the object of God's gift more than the method of procuring it.

7. James Strong, *The New Strong's Exhaustive Concordance of the Bible* (Nashville: Thomas Nelson, 1995), s.v. "coat."

8. Currid, *Genesis*, 139.

9. Strong, *Strong's Exhaustive Concordance*, s.v. "skin."

Throughout the Bible and throughout the ancient Near East, clothing is highly symbolic. The giving of clothing almost always represents an increase in status, an honoring of a person, or a receiving of an inheritance,[10] like when the priests were given new clothes that set them apart and showed their position (see Ex. 28:4, 39–40), or when Joseph was given his coat of many colors because he was loved more than his brothers (see Gen. 37:3), or when the father of the prodigal son draped his own robe on him when he returned (see Luke 15:22). Change in clothing accompanied a change in status.

What's more, the removal of clothing is often a symbolic statement as well—either as an act of humiliation or as part of the process of changing from one's former self into a new place of honor.[11] That's what we see here! God lovingly removes the flimsy, faulty, man-made clothes of leaves and replaces them with strong, beautiful, God-made garments of skin. He removed the symbol of their alienation and shame and replaced it with a symbol of restoration.[12] It is a picture of putting off the old, sinful self and putting on a new, restored heart as a child of God.

What's more, it was a symbol of God's renewing their calling as his representatives, his image bearers, on the earth. In chapter 6 we saw how the image Adam and Eve bore was damaged in the fall and how their, and our, ability to live out our purpose was destroyed. Image bearing is about imitating the character and nature of God, but if everything we do is tainted by sin, if we cannot choose God at all, then we cannot hope to live the lives we were created for. But God promised to fix that, and so, as a dramatic demonstration of his restoration-bringing promise, he

10. G. K. Beale, *The Temple and the Church's Mission: A Biblical Theology of the Dwelling Place of God* (Downers Grove: IVP Academic, 2004), 30.

11. Beale, 30.

12. G. K. Beale, *A New Testament Biblical Theology: The Unfolding of the Old Testament in the New* (Grand Rapids: Baker Academic, 2011), 452.

clothes his children in beautiful garments that represent their status as both his children and his chosen representatives. As G. K. Beale says, the gift of clothing here in Genesis 3:21 "appears to indicate a gracious reaffirmation of their inheritance rights over creation, despite their former rebellion."[13] This is huge!

Shame pushed Adam and Eve into the bushes that day. It told them that they were unlovable, unworthy, and altogether unwanted. It convinced them that God could never love them and would never want them. But God called them out and wrapped them first in his promise and then in his love. His gift was a gift of honor, a picture of status and belonging, and a symbol of their renewed calling as his image bearers on the earth.

Sin had separated them from him and made living out their purpose impossible, but God was going to fix it all. They were deeply loved, and their calling remained. God didn't just cover their nakedness. He didn't just cover their shame; he *removed* it. He reached into the miry depths of that shame and pulled them out to a place of honor. They were his beloved children; he saw them, loved them, and had chosen them still.

THE PROBLEM

Shame is one of those horrible things that affects us all, though it affects us in different ways and to different degrees. We feel it for different reasons too. Sometimes shame is brought on by sin; we're aware of what we've done wrong and whom we've sinned against, but instead of moving us to confess our sin and pursue reconciliation, it drives us away. It convinces us that we're not worth forgiving.

Sometimes, though, we feel shame for the things done to us. We start to believe that we deserved whatever happened, no

13. Beale, *The Temple*, 30.

matter what it was. That there is something inherently wrong about us that deserves to be unloved or uncared for. That we are broken and not worth fixing. None of those things are true, but again, shame lies.

Or maybe, as in my example earlier, we feel ashamed for the ways in which we don't measure up. We're too needy, too emotional, too loud, or too assertive. Or we're not enough. Not quiet enough, not gentle enough, or not holy enough. Sometimes we know that God loves and has forgiven us, that our sins have been paid for, but we still feel shame, not for our sin but for our need. We can get caught up trying to pay God back for something that was a free gift all along. But God's love is not dependent on what we do, and he's not asking us to pay him back.

We feel shame for different things and different reasons, but a common underlying factor beneath many of them is that we don't understand who we are and who we were created to be. Because of misunderstandings, well-meaning but misguided teaching, or even just our own assumptions, confusion has crept in. We've lost sight of our purpose, and the truth of God's love for us has gotten tangled into knots. Please know, I'm not saying that overcoming shame is as simple as fixing your understanding,[14] but it's a good starting place because shame gets to the very heart of our identity, and the Lord offers us clarity about that very thing.

We were created out of God's abundant, overflowing love and were created to be his image on the earth. It's our purpose! But the fall made it impossible for us to live it out. And while Christ has reconciled us to God, we still live in a broken world where sin and shame abound. In sanctification, the Lord is working in us to

---

14. I also strongly encourage anyone struggling with issues of shame to talk to a trained, trusted therapist. Getting help in this matter is one of the most important things you can do for yourself, and is so, so important.

make us more and more like his Son. Christ is the fullness of God, and we are being renewed to be more like him. Untangling the confusion and the lies and the misunderstandings is vital to living out the image of God, to flourishing.

Sin separated us from God and destroyed our purpose, but God's promise of restoration is bigger than that!

FREEDOM FROM SHAME

Adam and Eve were sinking in their shame, but God pulled them out, restored their relationship with him, and renewed their calling to be his image on the earth! Courtney Doctor once wrote, "Punishment is not God's ultimate answer to sin—redemption is,"[15] and I have to admit, I think about that often. I want to pull this truth close, to hold on to it and rest in it: God is a God of true grace! He's not looking at us in our sin and shame with disappointment etched on his face. He doesn't raise his voice, he doesn't belittle his children, and he doesn't tell us that we've let him down again. He is a God of restoration!

When I first thought about the level of grace in God's response, the depth of love took me utterly by surprise. How could he love me like that? How could he see all the things I had done, all the ways I had rejected him, and still want me? How could he love me when it can be so hard for me to love myself? Have you ever felt like that? Shame is pervasive. It sneaks up on us and settles deep and convinces us that our sin is too big for God.

But the beautiful thing about Eve's story is that it's our story too. No matter what you've done, what was done to you, or how great your need, God is gently calling you out of the bushes and into his loving arms. He's turned his wrath on his enemy. He's

---

15. Courtney Doctor, *From Garden to Glory: A Bible Study on the Bible's Story* (Lawrenceville, GA: Committee on Discipleship Ministries, 2016), 65.

calling to you, his beloved child. And he's removed your shame and wrapped you in his righteousness instead. Sin did not win, and punishment is not his final answer for us. Love is.

God's plan was never to burden us or keep us in line. Rather he calls us out and dresses us in his abundant grace. He brings us to places of freedom and invites us to flourish as those made with a purpose and covered in his abundant love. Because true flourishing is found only in him.

When we misunderstand our purpose to be image bearers, when we don't understand what it looks like to live that out as imitators of him, we will easily slip into places of comparison and shame. But God is beckoning us out and inviting us, as his beloved children, his restored images, into the glorious freedom of his calling. Through Christ's death and resurrection, God restores us and redeems us and calls us his own. He removes that shame so that we can live in the freedom and joy of his purpose for us to be his images.

SCRIPTURE TO CONSIDER

Genesis 3:7–21
Psalm 136
Isaiah 61:10

FOR REFLECTION

1. Shame can be extremely hard to think about, let alone talk about with others. If you're able, describe a time when you experienced shame. How did it make you feel? What, if anything, helped to pull you out?
2. Based on what you read in this chapter, write a definition for shame. How is it different from embarrassment or guilt?
3. What lies does shame tell us about ourselves and others?

How does the love that God showed Eve and the grace he demonstrated with his gift combat those lies?

4. Before reading this chapter, what were your thoughts about the gift of clothing God gave to Adam and Eve? How does the gift of tunics impact the way you view this passage? The way you view God? And the way you view yourself?

5. Eve was bound by her shame, but God rescued her and restored her to her place as his child. Read Genesis 3:7–21 and make a list of all the ways God demonstrated his love for Adam and Eve. How does he demonstrate his love for us in the same ways? What does his response to their sin and their shame tell us about his response to ours?

9

THE FREEDOM TO LIVE

*The LORD God sent him out from
the garden of Eden to work the ground from
which he was taken. (Gen. 3:23)*

Welcome to Pennsylvania!

The white script of the roadside sign flashed in the glare of my headlights. All around me were cornfields, dark and looming under a moon that was not quite full but full enough to blanket the world in its soft glow.

I had been driving for a while at that point, on my way home early from a college ministry retreat so I could teach Sunday school the following morning. Well, that's not altogether true. The truth is I scheduled myself to teach the next morning so I would have an excuse to leave early. I was a freshman in college, I hardly knew anyone, and going at all, even for a little while, felt like a big step. But, while I wanted to know more people, my what-if-they-are-all-super-weird-and-no-one-likes-me-and-the-whole-thing-is-horrible side won in the end, and I made advance plans for an early exit . . . just in case. But, as often happens in situations like this, I ended up having a fantastic time, so I didn't leave—not at first. I pushed back my departure until the last possible second, which is how I ended up driving through the forest in the middle of the night.

The retreat center was in the mountains: pristine, beautiful, and isolated. So I had driven down winding roads for a while before emerging from the woods in a vast sea of cornfields. There in front of me, in all its shining, reflective glory was the sign. *Welcome to Pennsylvania!* It was meant to be cheery, exciting, and welcoming. But there were two problems. First, I was heading to Virginia. And second, I had started in Maryland. Not only was I apparently lost, I was going in the exact opposite direction and was now in the wrong state in the middle of the night. Also, cornfields—everyone knows good things do not happen in random cornfields in the middle of the night under a gigantic moon! At least, that's what my panicked self was thinking.

Lost somewhere along the border of Maryland and Pennsylvania, I did what any young woman would do: a U-turn in the middle of the road. Three more U-turns later, I finally made it back to the retreat center, reexamined the map, and somehow managed to find my way home with enough time to catch a few hours' sleep before church.

As you may have gathered at this point, I am not particularly good with directions. I'm the one who somehow got lost every single week for an entire year trying to get to Bible study. I'm the one who looks at her husband like he's speaking a different language when he accidentally refers to the cardinal directions. I am a perfectly capable, competent woman, and yet I've also spent a great deal of my life a little bit lost.

The truth is, though, that the lostness I've experienced goes deeper than misread maps and necessary U-turns. I'm not even really talking about a spiritual lostness (a saved/unsaved lost), though that's a part of all our stories as well. No, I'm talking about a heart lostness. The sort of lostness that says, "Where in the world do I go from here?"

It's a deep sort of lostness, and one I suspect most people have experienced. It's the sort of lostness that comes when everything has suddenly changed. When plans or dreams have shifted. When what you thought would always be, suddenly isn't. It can leave you reeling and wandering and wondering where to turn. I know it well, and I thought Adam and Eve did too.

I thought that they were cast out of the garden to fend for themselves. I thought they wandered unsure of what to do or where to go. I thought everything had been stripped away and that they were left alone. I thought they were lost. But I was wrong, and that is very, very good news for those of us who have wandered as well.

WITH EYES TO THE PROMISE

We have spent this whole book steadily moving through the early pages of Genesis to see God's purpose for us and his heart toward us. God created humans in his image to be his reflections on the earth. We were to be imitators of him and to be his representatives. We were to fill and care for the world and everything in it. This is a high calling saturated with dignity and worth! But sin entered the world, and the image we bore was damaged; our ability to live it out was destroyed. God, however, was going to rescue his children. Shame had driven them away, but he called them out. What looked like the worst moments in the history of humanity were being redeemed and brought into the light. All was not lost!

God, the Creator of the universe, stepped into the story as our Rescuer and our King. But the story doesn't stop there. While all was not lost, it had been changed, and life could not go back to the way it had been before. At least not yet. And so we see in Genesis 3:23 that Adam and Eve were sent from the garden.

Sin had separated them from God; they were unable to draw close to the Holy One. And while God had addressed their sin and promised to restore them, there was one more problem for him to deal with: the other tree.

The Other Tree

There are two trees of note in the creation account. God created Eden to be his holy sanctuary,[1] and in Eden, he planted a garden. And in the middle of that garden were two trees, the Tree of Knowledge of Good and Evil and the Tree of Life (see Gen. 2:9). The Tree of Life, according to God's words, gives life—but not just any life: it gives eternal life. That would have been an immense blessing, except now Adam and Eve are separated from God by sin. And although he has promised to send a rescuer to fix this, sin is still a part of the equation. God will have to send his children out of the garden, out of his temple.

His reason for doing this is simple. God says, "Behold, the man has become like one of us in knowing good and evil. Now, lest he reach out his hand and take also of the tree of life and eat, and live forever—" (Gen. 3:22) When they ate the fruit, Adam and Eve *had* gotten a sort of knowledge of good and evil, and they had become more like God. But that knowledge was bought by a rejection of his authority. With sin present, dwelling in the garden near the Tree of Life is now a problem.

The problem, however, isn't that Adam and Eve might get eternal life eventually. No, it's that they might get it now. Now, when sin is still in play. Now, when they are separated from God. The implication is that eating from the tree will give them eternal life in their unregenerate state, and that is something God, for their protection, will not allow. As Bruce Waltke says, "In their fallenness humans must not participate in immortality."[2]

1. G. K. Beale, *The Temple and the Church's Mission: A Biblical Theology of the Dwelling Place of God* (Downers Grove, IL: IVP Academic, 2004), 83.
2. Bruce K. Waltke with Cathi J. Fredricks, *Genesis: A Commentary* (Grand Rapids: Zondervan, 2001), 95–96.

Sending them from the garden is an act of justice—the logical consequence for their actions. It is also an act of love as God moves to protect them. They will live forever one day, but not in their sinful state; he will rescue them first. But while sending them from the garden absolutely is an act of love, it is still hard. This is not a happy parting; it is a painful goodbye. God, the perfect Father, sends his beloved children away, firmly and decisively, because this is what must be done to save them. That doesn't make it easier, though.

There is so much grief here, and, honestly, it's OK to sit with it for a time. It's OK to lament what was lost. We should sit with Adam and Eve and look out at the world before them, a world shattered and broken, and we should weep not just for them but for us as well. The world they walked into is the one we now roam.

But we cannot stop there! While this is a grief, it is a *mingled* grief, because once again there is more going on in these verses than I thought.

The Reason

For much of my life, I had a picture in my head of Adam and Eve fleeing from the garden. Terror is written all over their faces, and they clutch each other's hands as they run, turning back just enough to see an angel as tall as a mountain wielding a fiery sword in their direction. It's a picture of fear and confusion. A picture of two people lost and stumbling into a dark, barren world alone. But just as I was wrong about the clothing they wore, I was wrong about this as well. For although God did send his children out of the garden, he did not do so with anger and wrath as I imagined. Instead, Genesis 3:23 is a verse laden with hope.

Verse 23 doesn't just say that God sent them out, it tells us what they were to do once they left: "Therefore the LORD God sent him out from the garden of Eden *to work* the ground from which he was taken." To work! I've skipped over that part so many times, assuming it was just the only option; of course they would have to work the ground—it was how they would eat. Or if I did pay attention, I assumed working the ground was now a bad thing. I thought it was part of the punishment, like making a belligerent child clean their room.

But that is not what's going on!

The word *work* there is the same Hebrew word used in Genesis 2:15 when God placed Adam in the garden to "work it and keep it." It can also be translated as "cultivate," and while it can be used to refer specifically to tending the ground, when it is combined with "keep" in the Bible, it is always used to refer either to God's people serving him and keeping his Word, or, more often, to the specific job of the priests to serve and guard the temple.[3] This is one of the many reasons theologians talk of Adam as the first high priest; God's command to him is the same as his commands to the priests of the temple. It speaks to Adam's priestly role in working and guarding Eden and his calling to carry out the cultural mandate by cultivating and filling it with God's glory.

Now, in Genesis 3, the fall has happened, but God has promised to restore his people both to himself and to the image they bear. He has called them from comparison and shame. He has gifted them with stunning garments, symbols of their restoration. And he has renewed their calling to carry his image into the world and reflect him by living out their purpose through the cultural mandate. But because of sin Adam and Eve cannot stay in the garden, so God sends them out with the command to "work" the ground. And then he places a cherubim outside the garden to "guard" it (Gen. 3:24). Work and guard are once again together, but whereas Adam was once commanded to do both, he cannot because of sin. An angel will guard the Tree of Life[4] from Satan,

3. Beale, *The Temple*, 66–67.

4. It's interesting to note that, in keeping with the priest's command to guard the temple, the cherubim here was not guarding the garden against Adam and

but Adam and Eve are still to cultivate and fill the earth with God's glory. God is calling them to continue to fulfill the cultural mandate outside the garden!

Do you feel the hope in that? It wasn't a "kick in the pants, don't let the door hit you on your way out" sort of send-off. God, in his grace and loving-kindness, reminds his children that their purpose remains. God has promised to fix all things, to destroy death and sin and to bring his children home. The image of God they bore will be restored. Their relationships will be healed. Eve has been given a new name. Their shame has been removed, and they have been clothed as children, as priests, of the one true king. They have been saved, but it is not a rescue that leaves them stuck where they were. God's rescue sets them free to be bearers of his image still, free to fill the world with his glory, and free to have dominion over the earth. It's a freedom that extends to us as well.

Adam and Eve may have lost Eden, but they hadn't lost their purpose. God had equipped them with his gift and then reminded them of their calling.

THE WHOLE EARTH

When God created Adam, he placed him in the garden and commanded him to guard and keep it, and then he created Eve to stand at Adam's side as an ezer, a co-laborer in that process. They were to join together to carry out the cultural mandate. And although he placed them initially in the garden, Eden was just the beginning. The cultural mandate was not limited to the garden but was always intended to extend and encompass the entire earth. It was to be an outward expansion with the goal of "extending the

---

Eve but against Satan. Adam had failed in his job to guard the first temple, the garden, and therefore the angel would stand guard instead. For a deeper look, see G. K. Beale, *A New Testament Biblical Theology: The Unfolding of the Old Testament in the New* (Grand Rapids: Baker Academic, 2011), 618–19.

order of the garden sanctuary into the inhospitable outer spaces
. . . spreading the glorious presence of God."[5] They were to reflect
the image of God to the world at large by imitating and continu-
ing the work he had done in creation.

While God was protecting Adam and Eve from the Tree of Life
by having them leave the garden, he was also reinstating their call
to be image bearers on the earth! Far from hiding in the bushes,
they were to go into the world and reflect the image of God and, in
doing so, bring order and peace and hope. Where there was chaos,
they were to subdue. Where there was emptiness, they were to fill.
They were to bring flourishing, and they were to do it together!

Adam and Eve didn't flee the garden, running in terror from
God, as I so often thought. They stepped out as those imbued
with dignity, created with a purpose, and with their eyes fixed on
the promise that God would restore in them what sin had lost.
Life outside the garden wasn't purely a consequence or a punishment; it was part of the plan. They were beloved children of God.
They were called to take his image into all the earth, and that was
what they were going to do. Their mission was harder because sin
and brokenness were present, but the plan remained.

For so long I misunderstood this passage. God's children
weren't wandering. They knew who they were and what they
were supposed to do. And they weren't lost. They knew where
they were supposed to go and knew the promise that God would
restore them. The same is true for us.

We stand with Adam and Eve before a broken world with our
eyes firmly fixed on the promise. God is going to make all things
new! He is restoring his image in us, and his calling remains for us
to live out his purpose! We are to continue the outward-focused
plan to fill the earth with his presence. This means that the invitation of the cultural mandate applies today. We are to continue

5. Beale, *The Temple*, 85.

filling as he did, bringing order as he did, loving and seeing people as he did. We are to pursue justice and create places of peace. We are to push back the darkness and bring his light wherever we go.

God's plan for us to live as his images was always an outward-focused plan! It was always supposed to be about expanding the borders, the peace, of Eden. He is restoring his image in us, and our calling remains until he ultimately fulfills everything with the second coming of Christ.

LIVING AS HIS IMAGE

The question is, what does that look like for us? How do we, as individuals with unique gifts and talents, reflect God? Well, one thing is for sure, we don't do it by working harder. Exhaustion, as they say, is not a fruit of the Spirit! Everything we've seen so far is that our purpose is not about what we do or the ways we measure up. It's not about looking like the people around us or appearing holy. Being an image bearer is about reflecting God to the world, and we do that by joining with others and using the unique gifts and talents he has given to us to imitate him.

I don't know what that will look like for you because I don't know you. But as we prepare to step into the freedom we have to live out the image of God, there are a few things we should know.

Know God Well

First, perhaps unsurprisingly, we need to know God well. We are images of him. That means everything is about him, and we are to reflect him. As we saw in chapter 2, as images of God, we were created to be imitators, which means the more time we spend with God, the more we will naturally start to think and act like him. Rather than striving more, we can sit at his feet.

Knowing God well means spending time with him. We read our Bibles. We pray. I'm not talking about quiet times, though, or a prayer life that's formulaic or legalistic, something to be added to your already too-long to-do list. Instead, I'm talking about a life marked by dependence on God and a heart chiseled by time with him. Reading, studying, and meditating on Scripture as well as spending time in prayer is so important, but there is no one-size-fits-all way of getting there.

I have struggled to have consistent "quiet times," a fact that has brought me no small amount of shame over the years. I've had to get creative and find patterns that worked for me, that brought my eyes to him. When I had new babies and very little sleep, my Bible lived next to my coffee pot, and I read it each morning while my coffee was brewing. Other times, listening to an audio version kept me in the Word when life seemed to be trying to prevent it. I've studied the Bible at the kitchen table, a coffee shop, our family room couch, in the preschool pickup line, and even sitting on the bathroom floor. How you do it will change, and that's OK too. We're in this for the long haul, and that means taking little steps and making small changes that bring our focus back to him.

Our prayer lives are the same way. Knowing God well means looking to him, being in communion with him, and conversing with him. This is what Paul was talking about when he said he prayed without ceasing (see 1 Thess. 5:17); talking to God— praising, petitioning, and every combination therein—is an ongoing, perpetual practice.

We are loved by the God of heaven, and he has invited us to bring all our cares to him, and so we can! Nothing is too small or too trivial to talk to him about, and nothing is too little to praise him for. Prayer may be formal, or we may pray with cries from the deep places of our hearts. Knowing him transforms us.

Know Christ Well

In addition to knowing God well, it's also important that we know the life of Christ well. While Adam and Eve looked forward to the fulfillment of the promise, we get to look back and see that Christ has come. He is fully God and fully man, the descendant of Eve who defeated Satan and made a way for us to be reunited to the Father. He is the "image of the invisible God, the firstborn of all creation" (Col. 1:15), "the radiance of the glory of God and the exact imprint of his nature" (Heb. 1:3). This means that when we think about what it looks like to bear the image of God well, we can look to Christ who is that image. As the very fullness of the image, as God, he lived out his purpose perfectly. By knowing his life, we can see what we are called to as well. We can look to him to see what it looks like to care for others, to love people and see them well, to push back against sin and chaos, to bring peace and create spaces for others to flourish. In him we see what it looks like to fill minds with truth and point people to the Lord.

Knowing that Christ is the image of God means that we can understand the spiritual component to image bearing better too. We can see that his command in Matthew 28:19 that we go into all the world and make disciples is an expansion of the outward-focused, order-bringing, and earth-filling cultural mandate. And while we cannot do all the things he did—miracles, for example—we can learn from him what it looks like to live as the image of God in a broken world.

What's more, because we know that Christ is the image of God, we can start to understand more fully that sanctification is the process by which we are being made to look more like Christ; in other words, sanctification is how God is restoring his image in us. This is what Paul is talking about when he says to "put on the new self, which is being renewed in knowledge after the image of its creator" (Col. 3:10).[6] In order to know what it looks like for us to live out the image of God, we need to know Christ.

6. See also Romans 6:4–11; Ephesians 4:20–32; and Colossians 3:1–12.

Know Ourselves Well

The next person we need to know is ourselves. Does that make you feel uncomfortable? It did for me. For a long time, I thought being humble meant not thinking about myself at all. And not just in a self-centered type of way! I believed being introspective at all was the root of pride. So, I avoided introspection. I didn't know the ways that God had gifted me or the ways he was inviting me to use those gifts. I didn't understand that he loved me and delighted in me, that he gave me those gifts and graces to actually use!

Far from being bad or selfish, figuring how God has gifted you is an important aspect of living out the image of God. This is in part what Paul is talking about in 1 Corinthians 12 when he describes spiritual gifts and says we are all members of the body of Christ. We are not all the same, and that's a good thing! But we must know ourselves to know how we can serve him.

Knowing ourselves means taking the time and doing the work to see where our skills lie. It means asking ourselves questions like: What do I love to do? What brings me joy? What do other people see in me? What do I see around me that I wish could be changed? What tugs at my heart and brings tears to my eyes? Such questions will help you to know yourself better, identify the traits that make you uniquely you, and will help you to start discovering what God is inviting you to do. And then try new things to see how they go.

I am not saying we should shirk all responsibility and go on a cross-country journey to "discover ourselves." I'm not suggesting we invest money or blow off the responsibilities we have now in an attempt to know the "real you." This is about carving out moments to consider who God created when he created us and then taking that information to see how we can use those skills to imitate him.

I am also not saying we should avoid, or quit altogether, the things that are outside our realm of gifting. Knowing that God has given us skills in one area does not mean we can ignore all other responsibilities to do just those things that we love; we need to be wise. But it does mean that we can, and should, look for ways to use our gifts to bless our families, our churches, and our communities.

Know Others Well

That brings us to this last point. Not only do we need to know God well and know ourselves well, but we need to seek to know others well too. Living out the image of God is about bringing flourishing to the world around us; it is about joining with others, for others. We cannot exist as independent, individualistic islands and still expect to experience the blessing that comes from living as image bearers nor can we expect to live out our purpose with the fullness we were created to. We must be in community.

Not only does this mean that we must know our neighbors so that we can be a blessing to them; we also need to know the body of Christ. Being active in the local church, in some ways, is not just a great idea—it's vital to living out our purpose. Over and over again, the Bible makes it clear that the local church is foundational to our spiritual growth. Through it we are encouraged and exhorted; through it we hear truth and find people to turn to in times of trouble or hardship. We need our brothers and sisters in the church, and they need us. Again, we were designed to live out our purpose in community.

UNTANGLED

I vividly remember the first time I heard that the cultural mandate was about more than just babies and farming. I was sitting in a seminary classroom as my professor lectured about

Genesis 1. All the students around me were typing away, but I just stared at him. I had made so many assumptions, missed the context, and gotten so tangled up in misunderstandings that his words brought tears to my eyes. As he talked about the outward focus of the cultural mandate, its application to all parts of our lives, its invitation to imitate the actions of God himself, he had no idea that his simple words were starting to set me free.

I had a purpose! After spending so many years hurting, comparing, sinking in shame, the idea of image bearing as my highest purpose in life was revolutionary. After all the exhaustion, here was rest for my soul. Can you relate to that? It was like taking a breath of fresh air after being pulled from a burning building. Like eating a feast after surviving on nothing but rice cakes. God's overflowing, abundant love had caused him to create us in his image. Being made in his image means we have more value and higher worth than I ever imagined—not based on anything we do, but based on who he is. And rather than telling us to look the same and do the same things, God has freed us to use the unique gifts and talents we have and to join together to bring flourishing to the world around us.

I still get lost easily. Not as often anymore, thanks to my GPS, which gets me to new places with minimal U-turns. But the deep sort of lostness that we talked about earlier isn't a problem for me anymore; I know who I am because I know who God is. Not that I don't struggle. I do. We all do. But whereas once I was bound by my shame and tangled up in confusion, I've been freed. I didn't understand my purpose, but now I have clarity. I didn't know what it looked like for me to live as the image of God, but now I'm slowly figuring it out and resting in him in the meantime.

Adam and Eve walked out from the garden loved, called, and chosen. Their eyes were firmly fixed on God's promise to make all things new. They weren't wandering, and they weren't lost, and we don't need to be either. We are image bearers of God. We were created out of his abundant love, we were called with a purpose, and we have been equipped to imitate him! We live out the image of God together and in every sphere of our lives. We imitate him at home, at work, and at church. We fill and subdue; we create and bring order both in the secular and spiritual realms. We have been called to bring the fullness of God to the world, and we do that by living as his image.

We have been freed to live as image bearers of God.

SCRIPTURE TO CONSIDER

Genesis 3:7–24
Colossians 3:1–17
Hebrews 1:1–3

FOR REFLECTION

1. Describe a time in your life when you felt lost. What happened? How did you feel?
2. Adam and Eve walked out of the garden with confidence, knowing who they were and what God had called them to do. Is that a confidence you've experienced before? How does seeing their response to his calling impact the way you see your own?
3. Think about the four things we, as image bearers, need to know in order to live as the image of God: God, Christ, ourselves, and others. How well do you think you know each? How could you know them better?
4. Take some time to think and pray about all we've talked about in this book. In what areas is God stirring you up to reflect him? What unique gifts and talents can you use to reflect him and bring flourishing to others?

5. Do you feel like you are experiencing the freedom to live as God's image, as he purposed, or do you feel like misunderstandings have tangled you up? How is he working in your heart to set you free? What would it look like for you to live in freedom as his image?

CONCLUSION

*Those who look to him are radiant, and their
faces shall never be ashamed. (Ps. 34:5)*

"Do you take personal checks?"

The man behind the gas station counter slowly shook his head. I wasn't surprised. I'd never heard of gas stations taking checks, but my gas tank was empty and checks were all I had. The cashier's eyes were kind, but that did nothing to stop the fear from filling my chest. I was stranded.

This was years ago. Back before I had a cell phone or a credit card, back in the days when I drove my grandpa's old 1982 Honda Accord and loved my old-school tape deck. I was a young woman trying my hand at being a responsible adult, but on that particular day, everything had gone wrong. What was supposed to be a morning training session for my new job had turned into a full-day meeting over two hours away. And I, not expecting this change and not knowing what else to do, had spent my last three dollars in cash on lunch. The end of the day found me tired and hungry as I pulled into a gas station thirty minutes from my house, running on nothing but fumes and fear. My gas light was on. I was far from home. And I was stuck.

"What seems to be the problem?"

The voice belonged to an older man standing next to the counter; he was tall and spoke with a thick Texan accent that matched his bolo tie and cowboy hat. I'd noticed him chatting with the cashier when I walked in but hadn't really seen him until now. Not knowing what else to do, I explained the situation: I had a checkbook with money in the bank but no cash, and I didn't know how I was going to get home.

A twenty-dollar bill was in his hand before I even finished speaking. He held it out to me, his face awash in compassion. To be honest, I didn't want to take it. My pride stung at the idea of accepting his help, so I tried to say no, to tell him that I would figure something else out. But he shook his head and pressed the bill into my hand.

"If my daughter were stranded," he said softly, "I hope someone would do the same for her. Fill up your tank; get home safely."

I wasn't sure what else to do. I was alone and scared, and he was kind and offering exactly what I needed. I nodded and closed my fingers around the bill. I told him that I didn't need much and promised to come right back in to give him his change. Minutes later, after putting exactly ten dollars' worth of gas in my tank, I did just that. But he was already gone.

What's more, while I was filling up, he had paid the cashier, leaving me with a way home and a twenty in my hand. The man behind the counter didn't know who he was, just that he'd been hanging out chatting for a while before I came in. Eventually, bewildered, I walked back to my car and drove home just like he had said I should, stunned but grateful.

Sure, there were no thrilling heroics or imminent danger, but that man saved me. When I could do nothing to help myself, he did it all for me. When I had nothing to offer, he was exceedingly generous. He saved me that day. But here's the deal. He didn't just save me *from* an empty gas tank or *from* a fear-filled afternoon. He saved me *for* something too. He saved me so I could get home.

FREEDOM TO FLOURISH

Once I was able to drive home, it would have been ridiculous for me to have stood in the gas station for the rest of the evening. Laughable, even. And yet, so much of my life has been spent just like that. Knowing what I was saved from, but knowing very little of what I had been saved for. I knew I had been saved from my sin, but I didn't know what I was supposed to do next. What did it look like to be a woman of God?

I didn't have a good answer. Oh sure, I had *answers*, but they weren't good ones. I knew what I was supposed to do and not do. I knew how Christian women should act and how they should serve and what they should wear. But underneath all those ideas, all those rules, ran a current of confusion. Was this really it? Did God care only about what I did, or was it possible that he cared about my heart too?

I spent so long trying to fit the mold. I worked hard to do everything I thought I was supposed to do, to be the woman I was supposed to be, but rather than bring me closer to the Lord, my efforts left me exhausted instead. Can you relate? To be clear, I didn't realize I had misunderstood his purpose for me. In fact, I thought striving *was* the purpose! I had no idea that his plan wasn't based on what I did; it was based on who he was. And I had no clue that he had called me to live out that purpose in a way that is extravagant and freeing.

Eventually, with the help of godly professors and teachers I started to understand the beauty of what it means to be made in the image of God, and I started to understand the glorious calling to live that out. God was setting me free from confusion and hurts and doubt. He was stripping away the comparison and the shame, saving me from them. But the truly amazing thing to me was that the more I understood his heart for us to bear his image, the more I saw that he wasn't just saving me *from* sin or from confusion or even from shame, he was saving me *for* life as his beloved child. For life as his redeemed image bearer.

I am an image bearer of God! It still sort of blows me away. How had I missed that for so long? How could I read the rest of the Bible and not see it? His love is overwhelming, and his purpose is almost unfathomable! His plan for me is huge and freeing! What's more, I have been redeemed not just so that one day I can be with him but so that I can fulfill my calling *right now*! So that right now I can join him in his work to fill the earth with his glory!

And you know, I don't fit the mold. I'm weird and quirky and don't imitate him in the same ways that many of the women I have admired do. But I'm learning that that's OK—more than that, it's the way it's supposed to be.

I love art and the theater and storytelling and superheroes. I sing loudly in the shower and dance like a fool in my kitchen. I laugh at potty jokes and sometimes burn the dinner I worked all afternoon to cook. I play computer games and snuggle with my kids and lead Bible study and teach children's church. I'm a geek and a nerd and a mom and a wife and a writer, but more than all of those, I am an image bearer of God. And so are you. However he created you, whatever gifts and passions you have been given, in whatever ways he is inviting you to imitate him, you are made in his image. It's the message I want to scream from the hilltops: You are loved! You are called! And you are being restored!

It's so easy to be tangled up in confusion and let rules become our purpose. Because there are rules, of course. God does tell us much about how we are to live in this world. But they are not the heart of his plan for us, and when we make them the heart, we just get confused. I know because, as I've said, I was there for a very long time. If that is your story too, I hope and pray this book has been an encouragement to you and that the Lord works to untangle you from any confusion and show you the freedom of living as his image—freedom to flourish. I hope that a deeper look at what was going on in the garden helps to unravel the misunderstandings and brings you hope. As children of God, we have been freed from sin, but not just that, we have been freed to live as his image.

AN EXTRAVAGANT CALLING

I love the first three chapters of Genesis because they are so much richer and deeper than I realized. When I was weary from striving and exhausted from trying to measure up, God used Adam and Eve's story to bring healing to my heart. He pulled me out of my shame, and where I was stuck in the comparison trap because I had misunderstood his purpose, he brought clarity and freedom. The truths of Genesis have been a balm to my soul.

I wish I could sit with you. I wish we could find a spot on a bench or at a picnic table where we could feel the breeze and listen to the leaves rustling. I would ask you about the woman God created you to be. I'd listen to hear if you are excited about that woman, or if she scares you, or if you've ever even met her at all. I'd hope you have, because I know how important she is, how important you are. I'd hand you a mug of hot apple cider or coffee and I'd want to know if you feel the invitation of God to be his image. And in case no one has told you recently, I'd let you know that God's plan to make you his image bearer is amazing—that you are amazing. Because you are. Because he is.

God loves us! Not because of anything we do but because of who he is. And he has created us with freedom to live lives that display him in stunning ways. Far from the exhaustion and the striving, he has set us free to be women of God: image bearers of the King. It's an extravagant calling! His plan for us is bigger and better than I ever dared to imagine. I want to stand on the rooftops and scream that we matter! That our hearts matter. Our minds matter. Our passions and gifts and graces matter! The women he has made us to be matter. And all of that matters because we are his image bearers.

We have been created with a purpose, a purpose that flowed out of God's abundant love. And where sin damaged the image we bear, God promised to restore it. Where shame and comparison bound us, he has set us free. We were created in love, are called with a purpose, and have been freed to live as images of God.

ACKNOWLEDGMENTS

When I first started writing, people told me that publishing a book is a lot like birthing a baby. And while I get that on so many levels, the truth is, that's far too independent for what this process has felt like for me. Launching a ship might be a better analogy, because it has taken tons of people and man-hours and help to get these words this far. For this girl who never wants to inconvenience anyone and who struggles to accept help, writing this book has been a good stretch, though a painful one at times. But God is so faithful, and I have been surrounded by some of the most amazing people who have imaged him to me over and over again and pointed me back to him constantly.

Steve, thank you for all you have done to make this possible. You have loved me well, sacrificed much, and sat with me through the good and the hard of this process. I absolutely could not have done this without you by my side. You have mirrored the unchanging love of the Father to me on a daily basis, and I am forever grateful that he saw fit to let me walk through this life with you. You are my best friend, the love of my life, and my partner in all I do. I love you so much and am so deeply thankful for you.

To my amazing, spunky kids; you are my biggest cheerleaders and my constant source of encouragement. You bring me smiles and hope and show me what it looks like to love unconditionally. Thank you for all your support and all the times you gave me space to write when you would have rather been at my side. You three are a joy to my heart, and I thank God every day for letting me be your mom.

To Karen Hodge and Melissa Kruger and Meaghan May, all of whom championed this book early on, thank you. Thank you for believing in me and in this message and for all you did to push me to keep going. Thank you for the emails and the phone calls and the ways you have reached out and prayed for me. And to Kristi James for believing in this project, for working with me to shape and polish it, and for putting up with panicked phone calls, oddly ordered drafts, and a whole host of other I-promise-I-won't-be-an-overly-dramatic-writer-but-oh-my-word-everything-is-horrible-and-the-world-is-ending moments. I'm so thankful to have you as an editor and a friend. And to Amanda Martin, who walked me through so much and worked tirelessly to see this project take shape; this book would not be what it is without your help.

To the many, many people who have stood with me and encouraged me and listened and read as I've walked this path, thank you. To my parents who have always believed in me, who raised me to know the Lord and sought to be his image in my life, I love you both so much. To my siblings, both by blood and marriage, thank you for being patient, for checking in on me, for making me laugh, and for giving me nights out when I needed them most. To Meaghan, Katie, Sarah Katherine, Kristin, and Abby for reading chapters, and/or praying for me all these many months. Thank you for not giving up on me when I missed meetings and couldn't attend events; thank you for checking in on me and bringing me chocolate. You are amazing and showed me Christ constantly. To Christiana Fox and Erin Straza, thank you for taking chances on me and my nerdy ideas, and thank you for making those words shine. And to my professors who taught me, invested in me, and demonstrated what it looks like to handle the Word of God with reverence and awe. Thank you all.

And above all, thanks be to God who had blessed me beyond measure and given me this precious opportunity to share this message. I am continually baffled that he would allow me to take part in this and continually humbled that he has.

To my readers, I pray that these words and this message would be a balm to your hearts as you consider God's amazing, precious, radical, life-changing, heart-healing plan to make you his image.

Appendix

A DEEPER LOOK

Wait, I thought being fruitful and multiplying was just about having babies and being married?

That is a great question, and you are not alone. The truth is, a lot of people today think and even teach that interpretation. It is a common belief all throughout the evangelical world, and it makes sense given that we know Adam and Eve were married at the end of Genesis 2. That being said, there is ample scriptural evidence to suggest that marriage is not the *only* context for the creation mandate in Genesis 1:28, and this is the idea I present in this book.

There are three main reasons why I believe that the Genesis 1:28 command to be fruitful and multiply can be fulfilled in contexts beyond marriage and in ways other than procreation: the command's context within the creation account, the broader application of the second part of the creation mandate, and the universality of the command.

First, let's look at the placement of Genesis 1:28 in the broader context of the creation narrative (Gen. 1:1–2:3). To do that, we need to talk briefly about the organization of the creation account. It can be divided into three main sections: the creation (the introduction in 1:1–2 and description of 1:2–2:3), the garden (2:4–25), and the fall (3:1–24). In the creation section, we see the six days unfold, and in them God creates all things. Toward the end of the description (Gen. 1:26–28), God declares he's going to make humans in his image, does so, and then gives them the cultural mandate. It's important to remind ourselves where this takes place, because there is a natural tendency, especially with the subheadings we include in our modern translations, to forget that the mandate of Genesis 1:28 was given within the context of creation as a whole and to start to think it only took place within the smaller context of the creation of humanity. We can easily start to think that verse 26 starts a new section or is somehow outside the creation account. But it is not an aside; it is directly connected to what came before. This means that when we talk about verse 28, we must do so in light of the broader context of creation, not just the context of a command being spoken to a man and a woman.

So, let's look at the context of creation. What took place in Genesis 1:1–25, and how does it shed light on God's command in verse 28 for people to be fruitful, multiply, and fill the earth? What does the context of creation tell us about the cultural mandate? To find this answer, we need to back up and look at verse 2 because, as we will see, verse 2 and verse 28 are parallel passages.

Writing on Genesis 1:2 in his commentary, Derek Kidner says, "God's normal method is to work from the formless to the formed. The whole process is creation. . . . Indeed the six days now to be described can be viewed as the positive counterpart of the twin negatives 'without form and void', matching them with form and fullness."[1] Kidner points out two very important things about this verse. First, verse 2 highlights God's normal pattern of

1. Derek Kidner, *Genesis: An Introduction and Commentary* (Downers Grove, IL: InterVarsity Press, 1967), 45–46.

working from the formless to the formed. This is how he does everything in the creation account. And second, Kidner directly parallels the "without form and void" of verse 2 with God's actions in creation to bring form and fullness. Kidner's point is that the pattern presented in verse 2 is carried out in the detailed account of the days to follow.

Later in his commentary, Kidner examines the ways in which days 1–3 show God bringing form out of chaos. He then looks at how days 4–6 show God filling the emptiness.[2] The form/ fullness—or subdue/fill—pattern introduced in Genesis 1:2 is extremely helpful in understanding what is happening in the days of creation and especially helpful when we consider verse 28. In verse 2, God is going to deal with the chaos and the emptiness, and in verse 28 he calls his image bearers to do the same. The linking of those two passages and the parallelism between them demonstrate that the command to fill the earth and subdue it is directly related to God's actions in filling and subduing the earth. God himself has set a pattern for humanity, as his images, to follow.

What this means is that Genesis 1:28, although spoken to a married couple and dealing in part with procreation, cannot be limited to marriage and procreation; it is bigger than both because it's not rooted in the context of marriage but in the context of God's actions in creation. What's more, the fact that God is speaking to those he has just declared to be his images supersedes the fact that he is speaking to a married couple. As his images, the man and the woman were to imitate him. When we put the cultural mandate back into the context of the creation narrative, we see that God's actions form the foundation and the basis for his command.

When we get to Genesis 1:28, then, the question is, how are we being called to fill the earth? For that answer, we must look

2. Kidner, 45–46.

at how *God* filled the earth—he sets the pattern we are to follow. When God filled the earth, he did so by creating all the animals, the land, the seas, the insects, and the birds. He created colors, smells, textures, song, dance, and communication of all kinds. In other words, God filled the earth in a multitude of ways, more than just with his children. And just as God filled the earth with more than just humans, so we are to fill the earth with more than humans.

The command to fill the earth applies to all areas of life, extends to all spheres of culture and community, and is both physical and spiritual. To be absolutely clear, having children is part of what it means to fill the earth—a big part. But it is not the *only* part. In the context of creation, filling the earth includes more than procreation because the cultural mandate is a parallel command that mirrors God's own actions in creation.

This leads to the second reason why it is unlikely that marriage is the only context in view in Genesis 1:28: the interpretation of the first part of the verse in light of the second.

The creation mandate in Genesis 1:28 is a blessing given by God to Adam and Eve, and it has two main commands: fill the earth, and rule over it. It's important to note, however, that while these two commands can (and should, in many cases) be discussed separately, they are still parts of one overarching blessing and should not be overly separated. They are parts of a whole. This is important because although some suggest that filling the earth can take place only in the context of marriage, I have never heard any commentator or theologian suggest that the second command—to have dominion and rule—is to take place only within marriage. Saying marriage is the context of the command to fill the earth but not the context of the command to rule over it, then, assigns two different contexts to two different parts of the same blessing. But we must be internally consistent with how we interpret passages.

John Currid writes with regards to Genesis 1:28, "This directive has often been called the 'cultural mandate.' *This reflects the idea that being fruitful and multiplying and filling are not merely commands relating to human reproduction.* Rather, they apply to all of life, including the socio-economic and spiritual realms, as well as giving birth."[3] The command to fill the earth is an all-of-life command not limited to procreation. He continues, "The concepts of 'subduing' and 'ruling' support the interpretation of this verse as a world-and-life directive."[4] Note that Currid uses the context of the latter half of the passage to inform the context of the former. He applies the same method of exegesis to both the command to fill and the command to rule. He makes the point that interpreting subduing and ruling as an all-of-life command (as most commentators do) adds to the validity of interpreting the command to fill the earth as an all-of-life command also.

The command to subdue and rule, which seems to apply to the whole of life, helps us to interpret the meaning of the command to fill the earth as well. If the context of the latter part of the command is all of life, the context of the earlier part must be also.

G. K. Beale, in *A New Testament Biblical Theology*, says, "Some commentators have noticed that Adam's role in Eden is part of the initial carrying out of the mandate given to him in Genesis 1:26–28. Just as God, after his initial work of creation, subdued the chaos, ruled over it, and further created and filled the earth with all kinds of animated life, so Adam and Eve, in their garden abode, were to reflect God's activities in Gen. 1 by fulfilling the commission to 'subdue' and 'rule over all the earth' and to 'be fruitful and multiply (Gen. 1:26–28).'"[5] Beale anchors the cultural

---

3. John D. Currid, *Genesis*, vol. 1, *Genesis 1:1–25:18*, Evangelical Press Study Commentary (Darlington, UK: Evangelical Press, 2003), 87–88.

4. Currid, 88.

5. G. K. Beale, *A New Testament Biblical Theology: The Unfolding of the Old Testament in the New* (Grand Rapids: Baker Academic, 2011), 32.

mandate in the creation work of God. He makes the point that we, per the cultural mandate, are to reflect the actions of God in creation. These commands are not random or arbitrary; they are anchored in the actions of God himself.

Many theologians heavily imply or come right out and say that the cultural mandate is anchored in God's acts in creation and our creation as his images. Many see the command to subdue and rule as an all-of-life command, but when it comes to filling the earth, they revert back to the context of marriage and family alone. I understand the appeal of seeing the passage that way. I really do. However, and I say this humbly, I also believe that doing so is exegetically inconsistent. It loses sight of the larger context of reflecting God's own actions in creation and requires a switch to a new context in the middle of a passage. If the command to rule the earth is not limited to marriage, it is unlikely that the command to fill it is.

I am in no way rejecting the work of theologians who see the command to be fruitful and fill the earth as applying to marriage and procreation, I am instead suggesting that we extend the first part of the verse the same consideration as the end of the verse and open it up in the way the larger context suggests. It is not one or the other; it is both.

The third and final reason that the context of Genesis 1:28 is not limited to marriage is the universality of the command. Most theologians agree that God's command to Adam and Eve is a command for all people everywhere. This was not a command for only the first man and woman; rather, it is a universal call to all of humanity throughout all of history and is applicable throughout all of life. However, limiting part of the cultural mandate to marriage goes against that. It limits the blessing to married couples. What's more, it limits it to married couples who have children.

Although commentators and theologians largely agree that the cultural mandate is a universal command, many, many women in the church today feel completely left out. When we say that marriage is the context of the command to fill the earth, the logical implication is that we are commanded to procreate. Thus, the command doesn't apply to women who do not or cannot have children or who are not married. It leaves them out. Or worse, it means they are failing. In this way, it is not a universal blessing; it's a blessing reserved for those who qualify.

This implication does not need to be said outright or taught from the pulpit to be deeply felt by women in the church. It doesn't have to be said to be heard, and tragically, I have talked to literally hundreds of women over the last few years who believe it to be true. They have been told or it has been implied to them that the command to be fruitful and fill the earth is a call to get married and have babies. They have seen the way we in the church often idolize marriage. They look at their empty ring fingers or think of their childless arms, and they believe that the blessings of the cultural mandate don't apply to them. That they don't matter. That they have failed. And they believe it because we have mistakenly communicated that the command to fill the earth only applies to marriage. But it doesn't.

I recognize that I am walking a delicate line right now between scholarly research and emotional anecdotal evidence. But it would be disingenuous of me not to mention the reality of what is being communicated, the logical conclusion of this position, and the damage it is doing to the hearts of God's daughters. There are women in our churches, in our pews, and in our lives who have been hurt by this teaching; there are women who have walked away from the church altogether because these hurts have not been acknowledged. Even without this point, however, my conclusion remains the same.

I would never suggest we interpret Scripture based on what we *want* to be true or because we don't like the implications of what is being said. Rather, we must acknowledge the implications of interpreting filling the earth to take place only in the context of marriage. My hope is that when we see the implications for a large portion of people (unmarried and childless), we will look more deeply at what the text is saying.

It's also worth noting that other theologians teach that filling the earth does not just apply to childbearing or exist within the context of marriage. Abraham Kuyper, most notably, was a huge advocate of referring to the Genesis 1:28 command as the "cultural mandate" because of its call to advance all of culture. Kuyper taught that being fruitful and multiplying referred to the possibility of procreation but that

> [filling] was referring to something more, the filling of the Garden with the products and processes of cultural activity. As they began to fashion tools, work schedules, and patterns of interaction, Adam and Eve would be adding to the original contents of the creation, and eventually, even without the appearance of sin, the garden would become a city, an arena of complex spheres of cultural interaction. In that sense, not only the family, but also art, science, technology, politics (as the collective patterns of decisions making), recreation, and the like were all programed into the original creation order to display different patterns of cultural flourishing.[6]

While I do not make the distinction Kuyper does between "filling" and being "fruitful and multiplying," the point I am making is the same. The overall call to "be fruitful and multiply and fill the earth" refers to both the possibility of procreation and filling the earth with cultural activity. It exists both within and outside the context of marriage. It is not either/or; it is both.

6. Richard J. Mouw, foreword to *Common Grace: God's Gifts for a Fallen World*, vol. 1, by Abraham Kuyper, trans. Nelson D. Kloosterman and Ed M. van der Maas, ed. Jordan J. Ballor and Stephen J. Grabill (Bellingham, WA: Lexham Press, 2015), xxvii.

I want to mention one more thing in regard to this issue. I believe the reason we want to see marriage as the context is *because* we see multiplying as pertaining to childbearing. We start with the belief that filling the earth must be about childbearing and work backward, inserting a context to suit. We are afraid of what might happen if we open up the context. Will we be communicating that God condones sex outside marriage? Will we be diminishing God's high view of marriage altogether? These are serious concerns that are worth addressing. The way to address them, however, is not to change the context of Genesis 1:28 but to take a deeper look at what it means to be fruitful and to fill the earth—to start with the context and examine what is being commanded in light of it. And this goes back to what was said earlier: there is a direct parallel between God's filling of the earth and his command for us to do the same. To understand what we are to do, we must examine what God did, and he filled the earth in a multitude of ways.

The context of the cultural mandate within the creation narrative and the logical interpretation of the command to rule the earth make it clear that the command to be fruitful and fill the earth does not *just* apply to childbearing and does not *just* exist within the context of marriage. To be sure, marriage is a part of the context of these verses; however, it is not the sole context. What's more, there are repercussions if we get this wrong. Rather than being limited to marriage and children, Genesis 1:28 is a gracious invitation for us all to imitate God's creative work of filling and subduing. It's an invitation to join him in bringing his glory to the world.

OK, but what about God calling Eve a "helper"? Isn't that just a marriage thing?

That's another great question! The idea that a woman is a "helper" only in the context of marriage is a common understanding, one that is taught or implied over and over again. Part of that is because, like Genesis 1:28, Genesis 2:18 comes up in the context of a story of a man and a woman—a man and a woman whom we know will be joined by God in marriage in just a few verses. Therefore, it is reasonable to see God calling the woman a helper in the context of marriage. And to be sure, marriage is a part of it. However, as with the cultural mandate discussion above, Scripture indicates that marriage is not the only or the whole context. Again, there are three reasons to consider.

First, although marriage is part of the context of God's creating Eve (God immediately presents her to Adam, and they are married), we must look at the preceding events to better understand the greater context. When we do, we read Genesis 2:15: "Then the LORD God took the man and put him in the garden of Eden to work it and keep it." As we saw from Beale earlier, working and keeping the garden seem to be directly connected to the command to fill the earth and rule over it. God, in other words, was calling Adam to carry out the cultural mandate. God placed him in the garden, gave him the prohibition not to eat from the Tree of Knowledge of Good and Evil, and then declared that it was "not good that the man should be alone" (v. 18).

Right away it's important to note that the theme of this section of Genesis (Gen. 2:4–25) is life in the garden. In this section, we see the events of the sixth day in more detail as God creates the garden, the man, and the woman. Throughout this section we also see a theme of image bearing as God instructs Adam to live life according to the command God has given. We start to get a picture of what life as God's image bearer is to be like. The preceding events of God's creation of Eve are not marriage, as we often assume; the preceding events are God's declaration that mankind should tend the garden. Thus it is in the context of carrying out the cultural mandate and tending the garden that God creates Eve, not a context of marriage.

Second, and connected to the context we just mentioned, we

need to consider why God created Eve. After the repeated line "and God saw that it was good" in the previous verses, the words "not good" in Genesis 2:18 are startling and raise the question, what was not good? When we start with verse 18, we see God's declaration that it was not good for Adam to be alone, see that God gave him a wife, and easily assume that the problem Adam had was simply relational. When we start at verse 18 and look only at what follows, we conclude, understandably, that his problem was loneliness or even singleness. But going back to verse 15 suggests that God wasn't responding simply to Adam's need for companionship (a real need in light of his being made in God's image) but to Adam's need for a co-laborer. It was in the context of God's placing Adam in the garden to "work and keep" it (v. 15) that it was "not good" for him to be alone (v. 18).

God creating Eve as an ezer was not just a marriage thing; it was an image-bearing thing. Adam had been given a job in the garden, and it was in the context of this job, this calling, that it was not good for him to be alone. And as we've seen, the job that God had given to him, and to all mankind, is a whole-life job, not just a marriage one.

Carolyn James points out that "Adam was alone in his mission to be God's image bearer and to build his kingdom on earth."[7] Yes, Adam and Eve were married, and God has a high, high view of marriage. And yes, as image bearers we were created to be in relationship with others. But the overall context of this verse is not simply one of marriage, it's one of calling. Adam needed someone "fit for him" (v. 18), someone who was entirely his equal,[8] to join him and stand with him to carry out the call to guard and keep the garden and to fulfill the greater command of the cultural mandate.

7. Carolyn Custis James, *Half the Church: Recapturing God's Global Vision for Women* (Grand Rapids: Zondervan, 2011), 109.

8. David R. Freedman, "Woman, a Power Equal to Man," *Biblical Archaeology Review* 9, no. 1 (January/February 1983): 57.

That brings us to the third and final point: the universality of the declaration. Most commentators who deal with this passage suggest that in calling Eve a helper, God was calling all women helpers. In other words, Eve was created to be a helper, and therefore all women were created to be helpers as well. The problem with seeing marriage as the only context, then, is that not all women are wives. Again, there are many, many, many women in the church today who believe, whether they have been told this or just come to believe it, that they are less-than because they are not married. They believe that this passage applies only to wives, and therefore they do not qualify. But in the greater context of the creation account and the cultural mandate, this is a universal calling that affects all women of all ages throughout their whole lives.

It's important, in light of the previous point, to note that God's creation of Eve was directly connected to both Adam and Eve's creation as those made in God's image. They needed to exist in relationship. They needed to join together to carry out the cultural mandate. Eve was a necessary part of God's plan to fill the earth with reflections of him and with his glory. Eve's creation as an ezer, then, is rooted not in her role as wife, but in her creation as God's image.

I am not saying that marriage is not part of the context. I am saying that there is a larger context of fulfilling the cultural mandate that extends to all women, whether married or not. Once again, it is not either/or; it is both. Calling all women "helpers" or "ezers" is an exhortation to all women to be involved in the life of the local church—to serve God faithfully where he has placed them and to work alongside others in carrying out the cultural mandate.

Genesis 1:28 and Genesis 2:18 are two key passages dealing with women (and men) and God's plan for them to be his images on the earth. I understand why some people view them to only take place in the context of marriage. However, as I have shown, I believe there is ample scriptural evidence to support their fit within the context of marriage *and* the larger context of image bearing and mandate filling.

BIBLIOGRAPHY

Alsup, Wendy. *Is the Bible Good for Women? Seeking Clarity and Confidence through a Jesus-Centered Understanding of Scripture.* Colorado Springs: Multnomah, 2017.

Alsup, Wendy, and Hannah Anderson. "Toward a Better Reading: Reflections on the Permanent Changes to the Text of Genesis 3:16 in the ESV Part 3." *Practical Theology for Women* (blog), September 30, 2016. https://theologyforwomen.org/2016/09/toward-better-reading-reflections-permanent-changes-text-genesis-316-esv-part-3.html.

Barrs, Jerram. *Through His Eyes: God's Perspective on Women in the Bible.* Wheaton, IL: Crossway, 2009.

Beale, G. K. *A New Testament Biblical Theology: The Unfolding of the Old Testament in the New.* Grand Rapids: Baker Academic, 2011.

———. *The Temple and the Church's Mission: A Biblical Theology of the Dwelling Place of God.* Downers Grove, IL: IVP Academic, 2004.

Brown, Brené. "Listening to Shame: Brené Brown." Posted March 16, 2012. YouTube video, 20:38. https://youtu.be/psN1DORYYV0.

———. "Shame v. Guilt." *Brené Brown* (blog), January 14, 2013. https://brenebrown.com/blog/2013/01/14/shame-v-guilt/.

Clines, D. J. A. "The Image of God in Man." *Tyndale Bulletin* 19 (1968): 53–103.

Currid, John D. *Genesis*. Vol. 1, *Genesis 1:1–25:18*. Evangelical Press Study Commentary. Darlington, UK: Evangelical Press, 2003.

Doctor, Courtney. *From Garden to Glory: A Bible Study on the Bible's Story*. Lawrenceville, GA: Committee on Discipleship Ministries, 2016.

Freedman, R. David. "Woman, a Power Equal to Man." *Biblical Archaeology Review* 9, no. 1 (January/February 1983): 56–58.

Gerstner, John H., Douglas F. Kelly, and Philip Rollinson. *The Westminster Confession of Faith Commentary*. Signal Mountain, TN: Summertown Texts, 1992.

Hamilton, Victor P. *The Book of Genesis: Chapters 1–17*. Grand Rapids: Eerdmans, 1990.

Hammond, George C. *It Has Not Yet Appeared What We Shall Be: A Reconsideration of the Imago Dei in Light of Those with Severe Cognitive Disabilities*. Phillipsburg, NJ: P&R Publishing, 2017.

James, Carolyn Custis. *Half the Church: Recapturing God's Global Vision for Women*. Grand Rapids: Zondervan, 2011.

———. *When Life and Beliefs Collide: How Knowing God Makes a Difference*. Grand Rapids: Zondervan, 2001.

Kessler, Martin and Karel Deurloo. *A Commentary on Genesis: The Book of Beginnings*. Mahwah, NJ: Paulist Press, 2004.

Kidner, Derek. *Genesis: An Introduction and Commentary*. Downers Grove, IL: InterVarsity Press, 1967.

Kilner, John F. *Dignity and Destiny: Humanity in the Image of God*. Grand Rapids: Eerdmans, 2015.

Klein, Ernest. *A Comprehensive Etymological Dictionary of the Hebrew Language*. New York: Macmillan, 1987.

Leith, John H. *Basic Christian Doctrine*. Louisville: Westminster/John Knox Press, 1993.

Mouw, Richard J. Foreword to *Common Grace: God's Gifts for a Fallen World*, vol. 1, by Abraham Kuyper, xviii–xxx. Translated by Nelson

D. Kloosterman and Ed M. van der Maas. Edited by Jordan J. Ballor and Stephen J. Grabill. Bellingham, WA: Lexham Press, 2015.

Pink, Arthur W. *The Attributes of God*. Grand Rapids: Baker Book House, 1975.

"Richard of St Victor on Love within the Trinity." In *The Christian Theology Reader*, edited by Alister E. McGrath, 203–4. 2nd ed. Malden, MA: Blackwell Publishers, 2001.

Strong, James. *The New Strong's Exhaustive Concordance of the Bible*. Nashville: Thomas Nelson, 1995.

"The Eleventh Council of Toledo on the Trinity." In *The Christian Theology Reader*, edited by Alister E. McGrath, 200–201. 2nd ed. Malden, MA: Blackwell Publishers, 2001.

von Rad, Gerhard. *Genesis: A Commentary*. Rev. ed. Philadelphia: Westminster Press, 1972.

Waltke, Bruce K. with Cathi J. Fredricks. *Genesis: A Commentary*. Grand Rapids: Zondervan, 2001.

Wenham, Gordon J. *Genesis 1–15*. Word Biblical Commentary 1. Waco, TX: Word Books, 1987.

Why do Christians—even mature Christians—still sin so often? Why doesn't God set us free? Speaking from her own struggles, Barbara Duguid turns to the writings of John Newton to teach us God's purpose for our failure and guilt—and to help us adjust our expectations of ourselves. Rediscover how God's extravagant grace makes the gospel once again feel like the good news it truly is!

"Take this book to heart. It will sustain you for the long haul, long after the hyped-up panaceas and utopias fail."
   —David Powlison

"Buy this book. Buy one for a friend and live in the freedom that only the good news of the gospel can bring."
   —Elyse Fitzpatrick

MORE FROM P&R PUBLISHING
FOR YOUR FLOURISHING

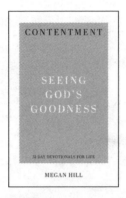

The world pressures us to fulfill our desires—but God tells us to master them through contentment. This practical daily devotional helps us cultivate thankfulness in situations that fuel discontent.

In the 31-Day Devotionals for Life series, biblical counselors and Bible teachers guide you through Scripture passages that speak to specific situations or struggles, helping you to apply God's Word to your life in practical ways day after day.

Also in the 31-Day Devotionals for Life series:

Anger: Calming Your Heart, by Robert D. Jones
Anxiety: Knowing God's Peace, by Paul Tautges
Chronic Illness: Walking by Faith, by Esther Smith
Fearing Others: Putting God First, by Zach Schlegel
Forgiveness: Reflecting God's Mercy, by Hayley Satrom
Grief: Walking with Jesus, by Bob Kellemen
Marriage Conflict: Talking as Teammates, by Steve Hoppe
A Painful Past: Healing and Moving Forward, by Lauren Whitman
Pornography: Fighting for Purity, by Deepak Reju
Toxic Relationships: Taking Refuge in Christ, Ellen Mary Dykas

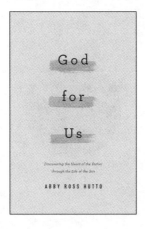

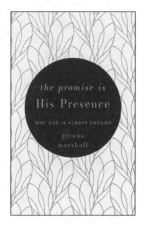

MORE FROM P&R PUBLISHING
FOR YOUR FLOURISHING

 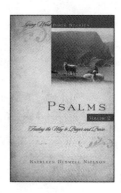

"Kathleen Nielson's inductive Bible studies have become standard tools for small groups reading the Bible together who are eager to understand what it says and how to live it out. These studies . . . teach people how to read . . . God's holy Word for themselves."
—**D. A. Carson**

Proven resources for deeper exploration of Scripture, Living Word Bible Studies provide effective guidance for groups and individuals alike. Each lesson includes questions for five days, plus helpful context and commentary, to lead to ever-increasing satisfaction, discernment, and delight in God's Word.

Also in this series:

Joshua: All God's Good Promises
Nehemiah: Rebuilt and Rebuilding
Proverbs: The Ways of Wisdom
Ecclesiastes & Song of Songs: Wisdom's Searching and Finding
Isaiah: The Lord Saves
John: That You May Believe
Colossians & Philemon: Continue to Live in Him
1 & 2 Thessalonians: Living the Gospel to the End

Did you find this book helpful?
Consider leaving a review online.
The author appreciates your feedback!

Or write to P&R at editorial@prpbooks.com
with your comments. We'd love to hear from you.